HAUNTED
EDINBURGH

HAUNTED
EDINBURGH

ALAN MURDIE

Frontispiece: *Major Weir's sinister house, shut up for over a century after his death.*

First published in 2007 by Tempus Publishing

Reprinted in 2010 by
The History Press
The Mill, Brrimscombe Port,
Stroud, Gloucestershire, GL5 2QG
www.thehistorypress.co.uk

© Alan Murdie, 2007

British Library Cataloguing in Publication Data.
A catalogue record for this book is available from the British Library.

ISBN 978 07524 4356 0

Typesetting and origination by
Tempus Publishing.
Printed and bound in Great Britain by
Marston Book Services Limited, Didcot

CONTENTS

INTRODUCTION

Edinburgh is a ghost-hunter's paradise. Stories of ghosts and hauntings have been enthusiastically told in the city and its environs for centuries, although the subject has not always been viewed as a respectable one

During the seventeenth century, a strict Calvinist interpretation of ghosts took hold, in which manifestations were believed to be an expression of diabolical trickery. This view was typified in an influential pamphlet, *Satan's Invisible World,* published in 1689 by George Sinclair, a scholar and polymath of Glasgow University. To claim a supernatural encounter might lead to one being branded as a witch and receiving brutal punishment. Although Sinclair stated that witnesses were not to be blamed for visions which came spontaneously upon them, others had not drawn such distinctions in the past. Certainly, Sinclair could not resist including numerous ghost stories and tales of second sight in what was essentially a religious book. In doing so he ensured that, of all his works, *Satan's Invisible World* is the one which is still being quoted today.

Inevitably, there was a reaction to fundamentalism and the superstitions associated with it. The atrocities perpetrated under their influence inspired a counter-reaction of extreme scepticism on the part of the Scottish philosophers and encyclopaedists of the eighteenth century against claims of anything not susceptible to logical or mathematical demonstration. Most influential of these atheist thinkers was David Hume, who famously declared an outright rejection of all things supernatural. Ghosts were dismissed as pure superstition and witnesses as liars, or at best deluded.

However, neither religious fundamentalists or atheistic philosophers were able to banish ghost tales out of Edinburgh. By the dawn of the nineteenth century, ghost stories were again attracting eager interest. Many great Edinburgh tales were joyously recorded by Robert Chambers for his *Traditions of Edinburgh* (1825), which represents the first book of urban folklore. The novelist and poet Sir Walter Scott cited a number of supernatural tales from the city and the area around in his *Letters on Demonology and Witchcraft* (1830) and his example was followed in turn by the first of the great Victorian ghost story collectors, Mrs Catherine Crowe. This unjustly forgotten lady lived for part of her life in Edinburgh and she recorded many chilling ghost encounters from the city and far beyond. These were published in her evocatively entitled *The Night Side of Nature* (1848), which became a best-seller and classic of its kind. Regrettably, her determination to protect the privacy of her informants at all costs means that today we cannot identify the whereabouts of many haunted sites with any precision. Mrs Crowe was also responsible for introducing the word poltergeist into English from the German language; meaning rattling or rumbling ghost, it is a description which fits many of the disturbances which still afflict premises in and around Edinburgh to this day.

A generation later the Society for Psychical Research began gathering accounts of haunted houses and examples of what are termed 'crisis apparitions'. These involve the appearance of a person at or close to the moment of death to a friend or family member. Although it was little acknowledged, these experiences were a class of experience recognised in Scotland for centuries as 'second sight', although the 'sight' was not confined to moment-of-death appearances but often involved a glimpse into future. Examples of this phenomena were first collected as long ago as 1696, whilst a study of over 200 modern examples was compiled as recently as 1999 by the School of Scottish Studies in Edinburgh. It is continuation indicates a particularly strong psychic faculty amongst native Scots.

Details of new ghost experiences in the city and its surroundings are reported continually. Whilst some property owners and custodians will quietly decline to comment upon recent manifestations at their premises, they are increasingly a minority. More likely, an investigator will be confronted by a host of sensational claims at celebrated sites, eagerly promoted by entrepreneurs since the first tours began in 1985. Ghost events and walks have become a profitable branch of the tourist trade in the city, with the number of tours in Edinburgh now eclipsing those of York, which was previously the UK's centre for spooky entertainment. Certainly, enthusiasm for old and new ghost stories is as strong as ever, and the belief or hope in another realm beyond the material sphere shows no diminution. A ghost festival of some sort has become a regular

James VI of Scotland presiding over the examination of suspected witches.

event at Mary King's Close and elsewhere, tours embark every night into cemeteries such as Greyfriars which are believed to have become centres of paranormal activity, whilst ghost hunters conduct all-night vigils in the hope of capturing evidence with scientific instruments. Modern witches declare their presence in the city, which would have been impossible in the past, and a curse of a religious character was invoked against an Edinburgh property company as recently as November 2005. From a scientific perspective, psychic phenomena have been examined under the auspices of the Koestler Chair of Parapsychology at Edinburgh University and psychologists have studied the experiences and responses of those exploring the city's haunted Vaults.

Probably above all else, it is the reinforcement of belief by continuing human experience which has kept interest in the subject of ghosts alive and ensured that traditional stories remain in circulation. Even folkloric tales do not deserve to be dismissed out of hand. Wherever possible, the earliest source for a story in this book has been sought. This approach has paid dividends, for it has resulted in the discovery of first-hand accounts from the nineteenth century of phenomena which had been wholly forgotten or overlooked, such as at Holyrood Palace and Woodhouselee. Over the years the details had been forgotten, with folklore and myth-making filling the gap. But it transpires that at the root of a number of 'said to be haunted' reputations were real experiences. In this book I am pleased to detail hauntings at a wide variety of locations and revisit stories old and new. My conclusion is that those who search for the paranormal in Scotland's capital do not do so in vain.

Acknowledgements

I am very grateful to everyone who has helped with compiling *Haunted Edinburgh*, for without their generous support and assistance this book could not have appeared.

For their excellent photographs, I would like to thank Dr Victoria Amador, Anna Pearce and Philip Hutchinson.

I am most grateful to members of the Ghost Club, particularly Derek Green, Lisa Bowell, Milton Edwards and the late Dennis Bardens for first-hand experiences and much background information on sites in Edinburgh. Among psychical researchers I would like to thank Tricia Robertson and Professor Archie Roy of the Scottish Society for Psychical Research, Dr Peter McCue and the late Andrew Green. Among folklorists, particular thanks must go to the Revd J. Towyn Jones, Dr Shari Cohn of the School of Scottish Studies and the late Dr Hilda Ellis Davidson of Cambridge. Thanks are also owed to Stewart Evans for certain illustrations and also to Duncan McAndrew, Geo Cameron, Robert Halliday, Dr Tom Licence, Norah Green and James and Ruth Rettie for various pieces of historical information.

Staff at Collingdale Newspaper Library, Cambridge University Library, Edinburgh Central Library, the National Library of Scotland and Balerno library all assisted in obtaining books, references and original source materials. Wyllys Poynton and Eleanor O'Keefe of the Society for Psychical Research helped track down references and files held by the Society for Psychical Research.

As will be apparent, staff, volunteers and guides at historic sites and museums provided much vital information. Occupiers at various haunted sites freely shared their experiences and recollections, as did the staff and proprietors of numerous hotels, pubs, guest houses and bed and breakfast establishments. Dr Victoria Amador also provided invaluable help in reaching numerous isolated sites and also helpful introductions to many local people with key knowledge.

Staff at Tempus, particularly Cate Ludlow and Laura Coulman gave invaluable assistance with editing and production and to Michelle Bird and my mother Janet Murdie who helped with proof reading.

Like many others, Major Weir, whose story follows, was said to have sold his soul to the Devil.

ONE

THE STORY OF MAJOR WEIR AND THE SPECTRES OF THE GRASSMARKET

The city of Edinburgh knew many eccentric and bizarre characters in its past. The eighteenth century had Lady Eglintourne who dined with pet rats and washed her face in sow's milk until her death in 1780, at the age of ninety-one. A contemporary was the slightly mad Duchess Catherine, who invited finely dressed ladies to walk with her and sit around her on a dunghill. There was Lord Lovat, who laid in bed for two years until he heard that Bonnie Prince Charlie had landed; 'Daft Jamie Duff' who loved to attend funerals and would run around the Edinburgh racecourse pretending to be both horse and rider and carried soup home in his pockets. These remarkable characters, and dozens more like them, were recorded by Robert Chambers in *Traditions of Edinburgh*, the first work of urban folklore, and later by Sir Walter Scott. On the darker side there was the notorious Deacon Brodie, who maintained an outward appearance of respectability whilst operating as a sinister thief and burglar by night, and the even more infamous Burke and Hare, body snatchers who turned to murder, supplying anatomy rooms until their apprehension.

If cases of human evil were not enough, there were also many stories of Scots dabbling in magic and meddling with supernatural forces. King James VI of Scotland, who became James I of England, had an obsessive fear of witches in his realm and a great many people were executed both during and after his reign. But in all the dark annals of Scottish witchcraft, there are few more ghastly stories to compete with that of the perverted Major Weir, who sold his soul to the Devil. The story emerged in the classic *Satan's Invisible World Discovered* (1689) although the author, George Sinclair, censored some of the more lurid aspects of the story of the wizard, including 'many things which Christian ears ought not be defiled with'. Weir was certainly no Harry Potter.

Born in Lanark around 1600, Weir served as a Lieutenant in the Puritan Army and continued during the Civil War as an extreme Covenanter opposing the Royalists. In 1649 he became a Major in command of guards defending the city and later worked in a civil-service post. Major Weir made his home near the West Bow and by day appeared an outward model of ultra-respectability, whom no one could exceed in probity and religious zeal. One source maintains, 'He became so notoriously regarded among the Presbyterian strict sect, that if four met together, be sure Major Weir was one… Many resorted to his house to hear him pray.'

Suddenly, in his seventieth year, there came an astonishing confession from the lips of Major Weir. His life had been one of sin and depredations so monstrous that they would ensure his execution; even by today's permissive standards Weir would have been facing a lengthy prison sentence. The confessions were so shocking that at first the Major was considered mad and

Witches dancing in the moonlight.

The West Bow, which Major Weir was said to haunt at midnight.

physicians were sent to examine him. However, the doctors declared him sane, forcing the provost to arrest him. The Major freely confessed to perversions which were distilled into the charges on which he was ultimately convicted, including incestuous relations with his sister and step-daughter, fornication with a maid, acts of adultery and even bestiality with a mare and a cow.

There was less certainty about the sanity of his sister Jean, who joined in her brother's confessions with even more sensational tales. She had been a victim of abuse by her brother from childhood but had then allowed him to continue until she reached the age of fifty, whereupon he had turned away from her aging body in disgust. Not only did Jean seek to corroborate the confessions of her brother, but she also added many fantastic claims including stories of sorcery and their direct dealings with the Devil. She stated that her brother's carved staff was a magic wand and that in 1648 they had been collected by a fiery coach which transported them to a house in Dalkeith. Here they learned of the defeat of Royalist forces at the Battle of Worcester, news which was not to reach Edinburgh for several days. Then by the same spectral transportation – invisible to other human eyes – they returned to the Bow. Jean also confessed to have a familiar spirit which she employed in spinning prodigious amounts of yarn. Popular opinion added its own bizarre elements to the confessions, averring that the place where Jean admitted to having first engaged in their abominable passions was a low hillside between Kinghorn and Kirkcaldy, which thereafter became barren and upon which no grass would ever grow. Another story holds that a few days before Weir's confession there was a spectral presence giving warnings in the close where he lived – near the site of Anderson Close today, adjacent to Cowgate.

During his time in prison, Weir rejected all attempts by ministers to bring him to repentance. Brushing aside their exhortations to pray, he declared, 'Torment me not before the time'. When questioned, Weir himself denied having dealt face to face with the Devil in materialised form; the nearest in his confession to a diabolical encounter was his recollection of a mere presence in the darkness. This – in comparison with the other sensational aspects of the story – seems a fairly pathetic manifestation for the supreme evil power in the universe but was sufficient to have Weir condemned as a Devil worshipper.

After a trial during which his sister-in-law gave evidence against him, Weir was convicted by a majority verdict. With there being no mitigation possible for his crimes, which were sufficient in themselves for the capital sentence, Weir was sentenced to death, without the prosecutors even bothering to proceed further with any of the witchcraft allegations. These were reserved for Jean, who was tried for incest and sorcery, 'but most especially consulting witches, necromancers and devils'. She too was convicted, the jury being unanimous in finding her guilty on all counts.

Major Weir was condemned to be strangled and burned with the sentence of the court being carried out on 11 April 1670. Before the execution commenced, Weir was again urged to repent and to ask God for mercy. Once again he refused to repent or pray forgiveness, declaring 'Let me alone, I will not. I lived as a beast and I must die as a beast.'

Weir was duly committed to the fire, together with his sinister warlock's staff. It was said that his staff writhed in the flames, as though alive, though this may well have been no more than wishful thinking on the part of the credulous and appalled spectators. His raving sister Jean next went to the scaffold where, as the report puts it, 'She resolved to die with all the shame she could, to expiate under mercy her shameful life'. Jean Weir treated her execution like a performance, further shocking spectators by suddenly tearing off her clothes and screaming obscenities. Today, given mitigation as a victim of duress, she would probably have received a few years of probation and a fine, followed perhaps by an appearance on a TV confessional show.

Following the execution of the pair, Major Weir's house was left completely shut up and abandoned to the powers of darkness for over a century. Sir Walter Scott, who knew the house, maintained it,

'...had a gloomy aspect well suited for a necromancer', although in a letter dated 6 January 1813 to Lady Stafford, who had been sufficiently intrigued to have gone looking for it, he recalled the building, '...as a sort of receptacle for half dressed flax,' though adding 'but no person was then bold enough to visit it after sunset'. For the Bow had gained a terrifying notoriety for being haunted.

Edinburgh tradition long held that Weir's ghost continued to haunt his old house and the area around it each night. A set of steps was said to induce a strange effect upon those using them, giving the impression of going down instead of up. Lights burned in empty buildings and mocking laughter emanated from them. At midnight Weir would be seen leaving the shut-up building, accompanied by the spirit of his sister, to climb aboard a spectral coach pulled by six coal-black horses. This phantom vehicle collected them every night in order to drive them down to hell, though in other versions they went instead to Dalkeith.

Eventually the house was occupied in the latter part of the eighteenth century at a low rent by an old soldier named William Patullo and his wife. They lasted one night in the place before fleeing. As the couple lay in bed, their room lit only by the embers of a dying fire, they were horrified by the materialisation of a curious animal apparition resembling a calf, which appeared in the fireplace and moved to the end of their bed. Transfixed in horror, they watched the creature place its front feet upon the bed and stare at them. According to writer Robert Chambers, the being did no more than stare at them until vanishing away. Perhaps not surprisingly, Patullo and his wife abandoned the house the next morning, and it stood empty for another half century.

Just prior to the demolition of the house, Sir Walter Scott recorded: 'Bold was the urchin from the high school who dared approach the gloomy ruin at the risk of seeing the Major's enchanted staff parading through the old apartments, or hearing the hum of the necromantic wheel, which procured for his sister such a character as a spinner.'

Even after demolition stories persisted of the haunting transferring to the Grassmarket. Other stories had the ghost of Weir appeared headless in the area, sometimes riding a horse, whilst other tales told of the phantom of Jean, her face and hands blackened and distorted, as if by fire. Yet others had the sound of the Major's staff being heard tapping its way across the Grassmarket, late into the night.

As late as 1947, the Edinburgh writer G. Scott-Moncrieff described Major Weir being, 'long the terror of children and of night passengers down the Bow'. But in the years since there appear to have been no further reports of these apparitions and noises, and a phantom coach reported in Charlotte Street is too far away to be the vehicle of the Weir legend. It seems that redevelopment has finally put paid to the ghost of the warlock. Lost, too, is the earlier house of Lord Ruthven, one of the murderers of Rizzio at Holyrood Palace (see Holyrood Palace, Chapter Three) whose ghost was said to have appeared on the doorstep of his old home in the Bow, an altogether mild apparition compared with the others.

The Last Drop Tavern, the Grassmarket

Although there is nothing to resemble the ghastly spectres of the Weir legend, the Grassmarket area is still producing ghost reports today. In an all-out embrace of gallows humour, The Last Drop public house stands facing the Grassmarket, a few steps from the site of the original scaffold. Between 1661-68 at least 100 people were executed at the spot, and a promotional leaflet for pubs of historic interest states, 'It could be that the ghosts of some... will be occupying

II

There's scarce a Month within these Years
But Witchcraft foul is done,
And many are the weeping tears
These Satan's Fiends have rung;
Though they sought Mercy ere the rope
Soon as the Judgement's read,
Who gainsays the Devil's Hope
Is all when they are Dead?

Over 100 people were executed on the Grassmarket in the seventeenth century.

the seat next to you when you visit The Last Drop!' However, it does not appear to be a former victim of the rope but the friendly presence of a young girl who haunts the popular tavern. Licensees James and Ruth Rettie have been running the pub for over twenty years, during which time both they and their staff have witnessed many odd poltergeist incidents, such as items being moved or falling from shelves (although nothing is ever broken). The most recent was a hot chocolate cup which moved by itself on Sunday, 25 February 2007, witnessed by Mrs Rettie towards evening time.

Mediums and clairvoyants have visited the pub in droves. Some have attributed the haunting to a young Irish girl 'wearing medieval clothes' by the name of Maria, but this contradicts her identification by other psychics as a murder victim from the eighteenth century. Ruth Rettie has searched local records but can find no trace of any such murder case. Regrettably these descriptions – which have a vagueness in keeping with many other pieces of information supplied by psychics – are not bolstered by any visual descriptions as no one seems to have seen any apparitions beyond a fleeting vision of a shadow crossing the bar spotted by Mr Rettie one morning. Nonetheless, both staff and regulars are convinced that there is a ghost present in the pub.

Another frequent and curious phenomenon in The Last Drop is that of staff hearing their names being called when no one else is physically present. Such experiences have been noted at a number of haunted sites in other parts of the Great Britain, including by a daughter of the licensee at the Druid's Head pub, Brighton in the 1950s. The same phenomena has also been reported in private homes, including the very haunted Beavor Lodge in Hammersmith in the 1870s and, interestingly, in Edinburgh itself at a private house on Blackett Place.

The Grassmarket today. (Photograph by Victoria Amador)

The White Hart Inn, where staff and ghost hunters alike have seen shadowy forms. (Photograph by Victoria Amador)

The White Hart Pub

Close to The Last Drop is another haunted pub, The White Hart. Investigated by the Ghost Club in 2004, The White Hart is considered one of the most haunted pubs, not only in the city but in the whole of Scotland.

Both romantic and ghastly historical events have been associated with The White Hart Inn on the Grassmarket for centuries, although the actual site of the inn may have moved, according to local knowledge. Although the current building displaying the sign was erected in 1740, its foundations are two centuries older with its cellars being dated to 1516. Here crowds gathered to witness public executions and condemned prisoners were occasionally given the privilege of a last drink before sentence was carried out. At other times the inn was the scene of happier occasions, providing the venue for marriage ceremonies for eloping couples, presided over by a resident 'priest' who performed a 'half-merk' marriage. Many visitors refreshed themselves before departing on stage coach journeys which left from the Grassmarket. Notable guests at the inn included poet Robert Burns who stayed for a week whilst visiting his lover Nancy Macklehose ('Clarinda') for the last time. Other celebrated guests include William and Dorothy Wordsworth, who stayed here during part of their tour of Scotland in 1803. It was from among customers at The White Hart that the infamous body-snatchers Burke and Hare lured victims back to their lodgings to murder them and then sell the bodies for dissection to Dr Knox at the Edinburgh medical school.

Which of this myriad of emotionally charged events may be the cause of the 'shadowy form at the doorway behind the bar' seen by staff over the years remains unknown. The figure has been seen by staff going down into the cellar: if they should attempt to follow, the witnesses find the cellar empty. However, sightings have been reported in the middle of the cellar of a partial ghost – a pair of legs – followed by a fuller human form. Since the early 1990s successive licensees at The White Hart have also seen a cold-room door violently slamming by itself and barrels have been moved from one end of the room to the other. Beer taps have been turned off by themselves. When such interruptions of supplies have occurred staff have immediately gone downstairs to put them back on again, only to find the supply disconnected again on their return. This problem has been reported at many allegedly haunted pubs, affecting casks of lager, sparkling bitter, some stouts and ciders. It usually takes three or four turns of the tap to cut off a supply from these barrels. Problems have also been experienced in The White Hart with gas bottles being disconnected, an operation which often requires the application of a spanner. Nonetheless, within a few minutes cylinders are reported to become detached again.

Such events have led The White Hart to being dubbed one of the most haunted pubs in Scotland. In an effort to study some of the mysteries of The White Hart, an investigation was conducted by one of Scotland's most active ghost hunters, Derek Green, who organised an investigation with members of Ghost Club at The White Hart, appropriately enough on Hallowe'en night 2004.

During an interesting night a number of investigators reported glimpsing shadowy figures for themselves, flitting to and fro in the bar. Members also sensed a male presence and feelings of cold, and efforts at séance communications produced subjective impressions of the names Sally Beggs and the year 1754 and another alleged female communicator who indicated a death in 1772, possibly caused by crushing. Derek Green considered one of the most significant events of the evening to be the unusual readings on a Gauss meter at various points in the investigation and a series of loud bangs which were heard on two occasions for which no explanation could be identified. Interestingly, similar repetitive sounds had been previously reported in the cellar and the cold room by staff.

It may be noted that similar reports also circulated about the former Les Partisans restaurant which stood near The White Hart. The building which preceded the restaurant was certainly considered a spooky place – a wax museum complete with its Chambers of Horrors. More recent stories maintain that the phenomena in the premises are 'on the decline' but there seems no diminution in activity at The White Hart.

TWO

THE CASTLE HILL AND
THE ROYAL MILE

Edinburgh Castle

Legends and ghost stories inevitably gather around castles. Edinburgh Castle, which has dominated the skyline of the city for centuries, is a classic example. 'Little wonder that the eye of every intelligent Scot is lifted with pride to the Castle on the Rock of Edinburgh. Yonder stands the most ancient monument of civilisation in this old grey city of the North.' So wrote Ratcliff Barnett in the 1940s amid suggestions that the castle harboured many ghosts appropriate to its antique and legendary history. Before being established as a fortress the site was originally the Chapel of St Margaret. Prior to establishment of the chapel, legend avers that it was the mountain abode of Pictish princesses and an order of virgin priestesses. When, in September 1853, a number of ancient female skeletons and coffins were unearthed at the site, many saw this as a vindication of the ancient tradition. Similarly, when the skeleton of an unknown infant was found in the castle walls in 1800, romantics had no hesitation in alleging that the bones must be the remains of King James VI of Scotland (James I of England) whom they claimed must have been murdered as an infant and substituted with a pretender, despite a complete lack of any evidence for such a notion.

The most famous ghostly legend claims that some centuries ago, a tunnel was discovered in the cellars of the castle. In order to discover its length, a piper rashly volunteered to descend into its Stygian depths, playing tunes on his bagpipes as he went, in order that those above him could follow his progress. The people above traced the sound of the music, but at a certain point along the Royal Mile the sound of his piping ceased. Nobody dared mount a rescue attempt and the piper was never seen again, the entrance to the tunnel being sealed up. However, for years afterwards the ghostly sound of piping was said to echo up from the ground and along the Royal Mile.

This tale proved to be not altogether without foundation as, in August 1912, an inspection of the floors and cellars of the castle led to the discovery of a vault and, on further investigation, a series of underground chambers and passages. These were originally believed to have been constructed as part of the palace or tower of King David II (1329-1370). Many tons of soil were removed during excavation work but no trace of the piper or his bagpipes were discovered. However, the castle Vaults soon gained a reputation for being haunted. Ratcliffe Barnett wrote in 1944:

If it were permitted to spend a night alone down there, one might hear weird groans from the prisoners' quarters, and loud laughter from the hall of feasting. The eyes of a sentimental Scot might also see the gallant ghosts go hurrying by, and feel a draught of cold air on the cheek as they pass.

Interestingly, precisely these types of phenomena were reported in 2001 in a series of experiments conducted by Dr Richard Wiseman of the University of Hertford, one of a series of mass ghost hunts conducted in the city as a psychological study. Dr Wiseman – who admits to being a sceptic – attributed the experiences to the brain misinterpreting natural phenomena in a spooky setting. He later carried out more experiments in the extensive South Bridge Vaults in the city.

Another ghostly legend is that of the phantom drummer, often repeated on the ghost tours which flourish in the city. Shortly before the siege in 1650 a sentry heard a slow beat on a drum one night and saw a headless form in the darkness. Calling out a challenge, he received no reply and so fired his musket at the figure which vanished. On reaching the spot where the figure had materialised he could see no sign of a body.

Opposite: *Edinburgh Castle, early twentieth century. (Photograph by A.H. Robinson)*

Right: *The State Prison, Edinburgh Castle Vaults and the dungeons below the castle have a reputation for strange sounds and eerie experiences.*

On subsequent nights the sound was heard by other soldiers. One version holds that the phantom drummer first played an old Scots march, and then beat out a tune known to be used by the English forces and finally concluded with a French tune. Eventually the sounds were heard by the commander Colonel Walter Dundas who presciently interpreted the sounds as an omen of impending war. Soon after, the forces of Oliver Cromwell laid siege to the castle.

The story of the phantom drummer underwent a revival at the beginning of the twenty-first century. In November 2001, kitchen staff were alarmed by reports of a haunting presence in the restaurant. The focus of the manifestations was a nineteenth-century soldier's tunic which was reported to be moving by itself. Kept in a glass case, the Royal Engineer's tunic was part of a display illustrating the story of Greyfriars Bobby, the dog who faithfully waited at the Greyfriars Churchyard where his master had been buried. In later years, Greyfriars Bobby had been regularly fed each day by the colour sergeant.

It was reported by the *Edinburgh Evening News* that during a function at the restaurant a worker had seen the arm moving by itself, as though being worn by an invisible person beating a drum. The arm was seen to move in this fashion three times and, being within the glass case, it was not possible for a draft or the wind to be responsible. Unfortunately, further enquiries were stalled as the worker was supposedly so terrified that he returned to his native France. The restaurant refused to comment further when contacted by the press, but another member of staff revealed that they had all been scared by the incident and was quoted as saying, 'There is a strange feeling in the restaurant and I blame the tunic'. Interestingly, the phenomenon of restaurant furniture moving by itself was also reported at the Witchery Restaurant, just outside the castle, one evening in 1986.

Rumours of other ghosts have also circulated over the years, including that of a headless man allegedly seen around 1960. This headless shade would at least not be able to smell a less salubrious apparition, a former prisoner at the castle who escaped by hiding in a dung cart but was detected and killed. Yet another story maintains that a phantom dog has sometimes been seen at the site of a dog cemetery within the castle.

If so, it would not be the only spectral animal to haunt the precincts of the castle. Perhaps the most intriguing ghost story concerns a dwelling occupied by a Colonel and Mrs Street who took up residence in a house inside the castle in the 1920s. The house was the scene of manifestations by both a human-like apparition on the stairs and one or more phantom cats. The details are contained in a letter from 1926 and preserved by the Society for Psychical Research after the Streets had moved out.

A phantom piper is said to haunt a tunnel beneath the castle and the Royal Mile.

The house possessed what the Streets called 'the shadow ghost' which appeared upon the staircase. Mrs Street found it intriguing, describing it as 'a shadow the height of a human being'. As time went on it seemed to become substantial, and once, before they left the property, it appeared in a room at the top of the stairs. The shadow ghost would sometimes vanish for up to ten days, only to reappear at the same spot. On occasion the shadow ghost also seemed to respond to its environment. Once, Mrs Street reported seeing it bending as if with curiosity over a brush and dustpan which a housemaid had left on the stairs.

Most fascinating were manifestations of spectral cats. In a letter to a friend named Caddell, Mrs Street stated, 'I did not see the cats so clearly as the people did in the Castle. They were never full face, always passing or back view, usually slinking downstairs.' The ones that Mrs Street saw were always dark, although her husband saw a grey cat in the drawing room. She added that, 'They were not transparent. I saw them by day and by gaslight. They kept close to corners of the banisters just as real cats would. The tails were certainly not up. They took no notice of me at all, no one else saw them except the one time my husband saw one.' Mrs Street also observed smaller 'things' moving along the ceiling of the house.

These curious apparitions eventually resulted in the Streets allowing a visit by an occultist named Taylor in an attempt to rid their premises of the spectres. His visit succeeded in bringing the haunting to a close, Mrs Street stating that 'I am not sure if Mr Taylor actually saw one, but after his visit to the house they were not seen again.'

Mrs Street admitted that stray cats making homes amid the crevices and outbuildings of the castle would also come into their house on occasion, 'So we had to be careful not to mistake real cats for the others. The real cats never came inside the house again after the ghost ones left.'

The Castle Precincts

A number of colourful ghosts are traditionally said to haunt Castle Hill in the area immediately around the castle. The most dramatic of these is a phantom coach pulled by black horses, the box filled with mourners dressed in black which supposedly rattles down the length of the Royal Mile. However, manifestations are not to be wished for since its appearance is said to be an ill omen, coinciding with disaster striking the City of Edinburgh (it may be a folk memory from the times of the plague in the city). Another impressive apparition is said to be that of General Tam Dalzell who is said to come galloping from the castle down the Mile on a white horse. Regrettably, no reliable witnesses have been traced or identified, nor for the ghost of Deacon Brodie who is said to haunt streets and wynds near the Castle Hill carrying a lantern. His infamous double life inspired Robert Louis Stevenson and the story of Dr Jekyll and Mr Hyde and is celebrated in the name of a pub on the Royal Mile.

Mary King's Close

Undoubtedly the most famous haunted site along the Royal Mile is Mary King's Close, a long-closed set of subterranean dwellings and passageways which were reopened as a tourist attraction in 1992. It is here legend meets fact: Mary King's Close has enjoyed a reputation for being haunted for over 300 years. Within its walls a seventeenth-century couple were terrorised by a series of bizarre apparitions. The details of their ghastly experiences were recorded in a tract entitled *Satan's Invisible World Discovered* (1689) by George Sinclair, professor of philosophy at Glasgow University. Sinclair may be considered one of the first scientific ghost hunters, a mathematician who wrote about navigation, astronomy, diving bells, barometers and the occult. Pamphlet literature of the day typically served one of two goals: entertainment or the promotion of religion. In both cases factual accuracy was not always the principal concern of the author. Sinclair seems to have written with both these purposes in mind, and his scientific background seems to have encouraged him to seek first-hand accounts and corroborate his stories wherever possible. Judging even by this literature the ghost story concerning Mary King's Close was an astonishing one, destined to be retold and reprinted many times into the twentieth century and also to feature on ghost tours around the city. A toned-down version may also be heard from guides who take visitors around Mary King's Close today.

As tour guides like to remind visitors, Edinburgh in those times was a filthy and unsanitary place, with the state of the centre being so deplorable that official business was impeded. Complaints went to Edinburgh magistrates in the early seventeenth century from the Privy Council, who declared the city was '...so filthy and unclean, and the streets, vessels and wynds, and closes thereof so overlaid and coverit with middens and with the filth of man and beast, as that the nobles, councillors, servitors and others of his Majesty's subjects [which] are lodgit within the same burgh cannot have any clean and free passage and entry to their lodgings... the filthiness is so universal and in such abundance through all parts of the burgh, as in the heat of the summer it corrupts the air.' Some half a century later a visitor from England described the buildings of the city as 'high and dirty'. It must also be said that Edinburgh – perhaps not surprisingly – was in later centuries to pave the way in public-health measures, though it was not until the close of the eighteenth and the beginning of the nineteenth century that these reforms began to take effect.

During the seventeenth century Edinburgh was visited twice by the bubonic plague; infection came ashore from foreign ships docking in the Forth. Although plague is not a disease caused by unsanitary conditions, the accumulation of rubbish and filth coupled with appalling overcrowding ensured a potent breeding ground for rats, the carriers of the fleas which were, in turn, host to the plague germs. After the second of these visitations, houses in Mary King's Close were abandoned and some fifty years passed before anyone reoccupied the dwellings.

It appears that in the early 1680s a law clerk identified as Thomas Coltheart moved into the Close as a resident. Whilst furniture was being moved in, a neighbour made the cryptic comment to a maid in their service that, 'If you live there, I assure you, you will have more company than yourselves'. Alarmed by the idea that there were phantoms in the house, the maid quit on the spot, leaving her former employers alone in the Close on their first night. The words of neighbour proved to be prophetic.

On the Sunday, Thomas Coltheart retired to rest whilst his wife sat reading the Bible. Raising her eyes she was horrified to see the disembodied head of an old man with a flowing grey beard hovering in the air a short distance from her. The eyes of the head stared intently and she collapsed in a faint. She was found later by neighbours who had come back from church, who revived her. Her husband disbelieved her story and after the evening passed without further incident they retired to bed.

The couple had not been in bed long when it was Thomas Coltheart's turn to see the phantom head, again floating in mid-air. He got up at once and lit a candle and began earnestly to pray. It did no good, for within the hour the spectre was joined by the floating head of a child and then a naked arm, 'from the elbow downwards, and the hand stretched out, as when one man is about to salute another.' Despite his prayers and entreaties for the spirits to explain their purpose the ghastly haunting continued – the spectres seemed to regard the Colthearts as intruders. More apparitions joined the throng, including a phantom cat and dog. 'Then was the hall full of small little creatures, dancing prettily, unto which none of them could give a name, as having never in nature seen the like.' Then there was a deep and awful groan and all the phantoms vanished in an instant.

Even by the standards of the day, the sightings were extraordinary, but it appears that the Colthearts were forced to remain in the property. Such partly formed apparitions or separated body parts are not unknown – it seems that some ghosts fade away in pieces or are only partial recordings of past events – but those witnessed by the Colthearts exceed any others in the annals of folklore.

A few weeks later Thomas and his wife were on a visit at Corstorphine when Thomas collapsed with a shaking of the joints of his limbs. He also had a vision of circling crows which he took to be an omen of his impending death. The symptoms proved to be the onset of a fatal illness; at the time of Thomas's death a friend living near Tranent, some ten miles away, had a vision of a cloud in his room. The cloud transformed itself into the shade of Thomas, causing the man to ask, 'What art thou? Art thou my dead friend come from God?' The figure moved its hands three times, as though in assent, and then vanished. The time of its appearance was later considered to coincide with Thomas's time of death, so far as could be ascertained.

The story is an interesting one, not only as an early example of a crisis apparition but as an illustration of the changing theological perceptions of ghosts, which had been a source of great doctrinal controversy in the century before. Whereas Catholics maintained that ghosts were souls of the dead from Purgatory, Protestants in the sixteenth century had believed that the dead rested in their graves until the Day of Judgment. As a result, apparitions could only be explicable as tricks of the Devil. Although Sinclair held this latter view, as illustrated by the title of his book, it seems his witnesses – who were presumably Protestants – no longer adhered solidly to this doctrinal viewpoint, at least as regards their own experiences.

For many years Mary King's Close was shut up and abandoned, though not totally forgotten as has sometimes been claimed. It may be that the belief in the apparitions was a factor in the closure of the Close; certainly the fear that the plague would break out again was long held in the city. Right into the nineteenth century, at Beth's Wynd, old wives believed that the plague would burst forth anew if ever certain ancient cellars were opened.

Fortunately, no disasters accompanied the formal reopening of Mary King's Close in 1992. Initially reopened under the auspices of the city council, the site was later privatised. Aside from the question of ghosts, it makes for one of the most interesting walking tours available in the centre of the city, allowing a unique view into the troglodyte world which existed beneath old Edinburgh.

A Japanese psychic who visited the Close in 1993 maintained that it was haunted by the spirit of a little girl. Guides at the site confirmed in mid-February 2007 that one of the members of staff had recently had strange experiences. A male guide had been accompanying a party of school children around the tunnels and glimpsed the figure of a young boy disappearing around a corner. Thinking that one of his charges had slipped away, he set off in pursuit – only to discover that no one was there. He was forced to conclude he had seen a phantom boy from an earlier age.

Above left: *The subterranean Mary King's Close, which has enjoyed a reputation for being haunted for over 300 years. (Photograph by Alicia Conde)*

Above right: *Fantastic creatures were witnessed by the Colthearts in Mary King's Close.*

Right: *'...small little creatures, dancing prettily, unto which none could give a name, as having never in nature seen the like.'*

Meanwhile, the story of the little ghost girl lives on. Although there was no way of corroborating the claim, the story of the phantom child of Mary King's Close has predictably proved of infinitely greater appeal to modern sentiment than a cavern filled with the decapitated and dismembered apparitions of plague victims. As a consequence, many visitors purport to leave gifts for the presumed spirit girl, a trend which seems to be accelerating. It appears a number of visitors have been so moved that they have donated dolls, toy characters and teddy bears; what a putative spirit child of the seventeenth century would make of a Westlife pop CD remains a source of speculation. Seeing these offerings reminds one of the persistence in the belief in spirits and observing the toys piled up in the flickering candlelight, one is reminded of the Colthearts' vision, 'of small little creatures, dancing prettily, unto which none of them could give a name, as having never in nature seen the like…'

The Mitre Pub, The Royal Mile

Set along the Royal Mile, this busy pub has been the scene of ghostly phenomena for decades, the most recent being strange electrical incidents reported in 1993. The name of the pub commemorates Archbishop John Spottiswode of St Andrews (1565-1639), who made the building his city-centre home and who today reputedly returns to haunt rooms in the tavern.

Spottiswode has been described by historians as the chief inquisitor for the Anglican Church in Scotland, a clergyman more faithful to earthly monarchs than the Church he headed. Certainly, Archbishop Spottiswode ensured that the religious wishes of King James VI were followed by the Church, but initially he seemed less enthusiastic about imposing the line of his successor King Charles I, aware of suspicions that the ill-fated monarch was a secret Catholic, intent on watering down the Protestant faith in his realm. His initial clash was with the Archbishop of Canterbury, to whom Spottiswode refused to give precedence at the funeral of Charles's father. However, within a few years he resumed his role as the theological representative of the Crown north of the Border. Eventually, it was his reluctant introduction of a new liturgy decreed by Charles I for use in Scotland which led to his downfall. The new liturgy provoked strong and angry opposition, which resulted in Spottiswode procuring a court warrant to force it upon unwilling congregations. The result was a riot at St Giles' church in 1637 and the rise of the Covenant movement demanding complete religious freedom from the Crown. The national Covenant was signed at Greyfriars church the following year.

Such was the growing opposition that Spottiswode was forced to flee to Newcastle, fearing for his life. In his absence, his opponents took the opportunity to depose him from his post of Archbishop by the unanimous vote of the religious assembly. They also denounced him for sinful practices. The Assembly found him guilty on a range of colourful charges, of profaning the Sabbath by 'carding, diceing, riding through the country all day, tippling and drinking in taverns until midnight, falsifying the Acts of the Aberdeen Assembly, lying and slandering the old assembly and covenant in his wicked book, of adultery, incest, sacrilege and frequent simony', the last being the Catholic practice of selling ecclesiastical posts. On learning of the resolutions of the Assembly, Spottiswode hastened to London but succumbed to a fever he had contracted in Newcastle in November 1638 and was buried in Westminster Abbey.

Tradition holds that before his flight Spottiswode bricked up his ceremonial regalia in his home. Somewhere within the walls of The Mitre pub is said to lay hidden Spottiswode's episcopal chair, whilst his ghost is said to make periodic returns and has been blamed for odd incidents over the years. It must be said that refurbishment and modernisation of the pub have failed to find

The Mitre pub, said to be haunted by Archbishop Spottiswode, whose chair is said to lie buried in the walls.

The cellar of The Mitre public house.

the chair but there is no doubt that the most recent changes have attracted the disapproval of many Edinburgh people, amid claims that the manifestations stem from the irate shade of the Archbishop. Given that the allegations made against him by the Covenanters included drunkenness, he might well be thought to have a spiritual axe to grind against his old home being used as a pub!

In reality, there have been no firm sightings identifying the Archbishop and the haunting presence at The Mitre behaves in the routine way of so many other pub ghosts. Strange phenomena were reported by the manager Ian Wilkie in 1993 when electricians reported sensations like electrical shocks, even though all power to the building had been disconnected. It seems the ghost was also able to unleash energy and apply force in other ways. An engineer installing a speaker for a juke box felt a push from behind: turning round, he found no one there. On another occasion, a swivel chair close to the cellar was seen by a workman to be spinning round of its own accord. These accounts came some twenty years after staff at the pub reported that doors opened and shut by themselves, bottles jumped off from the shelves and drinking glasses moved around without human assistance. The duration of these disturbances suggests that – unlike many poltergeists – manifestations at The Mitre are place-centred rather than focused upon a particular person as is often the case. Informed ghost hunters will also note the existence of standard ghostly phenomena encountered in pubs across the British Isles – one begins to wonder if there is such a thing as 'haunted pub syndrome'!

Like many city-centre pubs The Mitre has had a high turnover of staff, and employees in 2007 claim no direct experiences beyond a creepy sensation in one of the two cellars. On descending down to the cellar area, the second of the cellar rooms was felt to have a noticeably unpleasant atmosphere, comparable to a feeling that the air was 'too thick'. This impression was also shared by Dr Victoria Amador in February 2007 on visiting the cellar and may indicate a presence.

The Museum of Childhood, 42 High Street

The poet Norman MacCaig wrote a verse dedicated to the ghosts of the High Street in 1955 containing the lines:

> Their tales of deaths and treacheries, and where
> A tall dissolving ghost shrieks in the dark
> Old history greets you with a Bedlam stare

Yet these sentiments would hardly be appropriate to the haunting of the charming Museum of Childhood. The museum was founded in 1955 by a local councillor named Patrick Murray. Curiously, according to an oft-quoted Edinburgh tradition repeated in the guide book, the founder was not a fan of children but nonetheless started the first museum dedicated to them. Four floors contain dolls, toys and other childhood games and ephemera. With cassette recordings it has been dubbed 'the noisiest museum in the world'.

It is less well known that Patrick Murray considered the building haunted by strange sounds. He reported hearing footsteps on the floor above his office, experienced a feeling of being watched and heard laughter and whispering coming from darkened rooms known to be empty. Other stories – perhaps surprisingly – tell of the sounds of a child crying.

Today staff at the Museum express the view that the stories have been exaggerated by loquacious guides on ghost tours around the city, but it may be noted that the stories date from before the rise in ghost tours as popular entertainment.

Above: *A plaque on the Scottish Parliament building.*

Left: *A phantom monk haunted a civil servant's home in the 1970s.*

The High Street

'The apparition is tall and wears long dark robes. His head is covered in a hood,' was the description calmly supplied in July 1972 by thirty-five-year-old civil servant James Lightbody of the phantom which was regularly haunting his home on the High Street. James Lightbody had lived in the property for nearly four years when the manifestations suddenly commenced and as a result every visitor to his home was told about them. 'If you see a ghost walking about don't start screaming – he won't harm you,' Mr Lightbody assured them. But not everyone had found the experience a conducive one, and some friends and relatives had 'turned white' at the sight of a figure disappearing through closed doors and into walls when visiting his house. The most common place for the form to appear was by the front door.

Phenomena in the property were not confined to the apparition and, in common with other haunted houses, Mr Lightbody reported lights going on and off. Rooms would also turn cold and keys would mysteriously turn in doors. The ghostly activity was attributed to the building standing upon a site which was used as a monastic house some 700 years previously. Despite these odd incidents, Mr Lightbody considered the presence to be a friendly one, saying 'I've never had any bad luck since he appeared.'

The phantom's appearance and the fact that the building reputedly stood on the site of priory led inescapably to the conclusion that his phantom visitor had to be a monk. Alternatively, the figure might be one of the brethren who has slipped away from Holyrood Abbey, the poignant ruins of which lie adjacent to Holyrood Palace at the end of the Royal Mile.

The Canongate, traditionally haunted by a female phantom prophesying fire.

Canongate

The Canongate area which links the route from the castle with the grounds of Holyrood Palace is steeped in history and drama. It contains the historic Tolbooth Prison, now a local museum containing the exhibition 'People's Story', dedicated to the ordinary people of the city, and the Edinburgh Museum. The area was the setting for riotous events in James Hogg's novel *Memoirs of a Justified Sinner*. A lover of the supernatural and uncanny, Hogg would doubtless have been well-versed in some of the supernatural stories of the area.

In past centuries the Canongate was reputedly haunted by the figure of a woman who would cry out, 'Once burned! Twice burned! Next time I will scare you all!' She was reputed to be the spectre of the daughter of a wealthy family who once occupied a large house on the Canongate. She gave birth to an infant in mysterious circumstances, and the little that was known of the matter came from the testimony of a certain minister who was taken at gunpoint into the building to say prayers for the dying. On seeing that the lady did not appear to be at risk he was ordered to say the prayers and then ushered from the building, a bag of gold being thrust into his hands. As he departed there was a sound like a gunshot and he was warned to tell no one what had occurred. The minister returned home a deeply troubled man and for fear of the consequences resolved to tell no one until, a short while later, his servant entered and told him that a large house at the head of the Canongate was burning down and that the daughter of the owner had perished in the blaze.

Left: *The Canongate.*

Opposite: *The Tolbooth Tavern. (Photograph by Victoria Amador, as is the photograph overleaf)*

In due course, the minister died and new buildings were erected on the site but some years later a fire broke out. During the conflagration the form of the young woman appeared, crying out, 'Once burned! Twice burned! Next time I will scare you all!' So fervent was the belief in the apparition and so great the concern of the dire implications of its warning that as late as the beginning of the nineteenth century, 'on a fire breaking out, and seeming to approach the fatal spot, there was a good deal of anxiety testified lest the apparition should make good her denunciation.'

There appear to be no recent sightings of any female apparition but there are modern reports of a male ghost. In his book *Scottish Ghost Stories* (1996), James Robertson describes the Canongate being haunted by a tall figure, dressed in black, seen furtively moving down the street. He records a sighting by a witness named Tom Goring in the 1980s. One Sunday in January he was walking down Canongate with his wife and spotted the figure. As they drew level with the figure it vanished; whereupon Mr Goring discovered his wife had been unable to see it at all. James Robertson raises the possibility that the apparition might be that of John Kello, a seventeenth-century preacher who murdered his wife and unsuccessfully attempted to disguise her death as suicide, but equally it could be that of any of the many thousands who lived and died in the Canongate area over the centuries.

A veiled phantom lady dressed in black silk haunted Chessel's Court, off the Canongate. (The story was given to James Bone for his book *The Perambulator in Edinburgh* by a member of the Gordon family.) Strange breathing sounds were also heard just outside a bedroom door. According to tradition the manifestations were caused by a woman who had hanged herself in the property.

The Tolbooth Tavern

At No. 167 Canongate stands the Tolbooth Tavern, another monument proud of its ghostly associations. Built in 1591, the building has been used as a court and a jail in its history, becoming an inn for first time in 1820 and undergoing restoration in 1879. The inn happily embraces its haunted reputation, though its ghost is another example of the invisible poltergeist antics which tend to plague pubs and inns throughout the British Isles and seem to be particularly prevalent in Edinburgh. Staff maintain that the entity at the Tolbooth Tavern concentrates its efforts in the back of the pub, used primarily for dining, and specialises in knocking over bottles and glasses.

These events were confirmed in February 2007 by a lady who has been visiting the Tolbooth Tavern for eighteen years, and who has witnessed books jumping from an upper shelf in the front bar. Staff also report having seen apparitions in their peripheral vision, usually having a fleeting glimpse of a form passing a particular upstairs door when it is left open. Their experiences are in keeping with the tradition that psychic activity is best glimpsed from the corner of the eye. If ghost manifestations involve the normal light spectrum there may even be a physiological basis for this experience in the structure of the eye, as certain sensitive portions are set to the side of the retina, and respond better to conditions of low illumination and fainter light sources than cells at the front.

One customer has been particularly disturbed by the appearance of two gentlemen in what were described as 'old-fashioned military costumes', but the regular staff consider their spectral visitors friendly.

THREE

HOLYROOD PALACE TO ARTHUR'S SEAT

Standing graciously beyond the far end of the Royal Mile is the historic palace of Holyrood, the official home to the royal family when in Edinburgh. First established as a royal residence by King James V of Scotland and his daughter Mary Queen of Scots, it was later adapted by King Charles I and remains one of the most impressive buildings in Scotland.

As with Edinburgh Castle, many feel that an ancient building such as Holyrood Palace deserves to be haunted. The corridors of the palace are said to be periodically prowled by a Grey Lady and unexplained footsteps are allegedly heard, though details are scarce as to when they were first experienced. The idea that the palace really should have ghosts seems to have arisen in the early Victorian era. In 1838 the Revd Thomas Frognall Dibdin wrote 'Where does the spirit of the unfortunate Mary seem so emphatically to linger as here? Where could its haunts find a more general sympathy than within these old abbey walls?' For his part, during a tour of the palace the Revd Dibdin had a strong impression of the murder of Rizzio, the lover of Mary, Queen of Scots, in the rooms where the brutal assassination reputedly took place. Of course, this could have been auto-suggestion or a romantic imagination being given liberty to wander, but it is interesting to note similar sensations being reported nearly 140 years later.

Certainly, there have been well-authenticated accounts of manifestations at Holyrood Palace stretching back over a century, the most notable coming from Lady Tweedale, the wife of the Lord High Commissioner, at the palace in 1890. Lady Tweedale's experiences were recorded in interviews conducted in July 1896 by the great psychical researcher Frederic Myers, one of the founders of the Society for Psychical Research. The details are published here for the first time in book form.

From childhood Lady Tweedale underwent a number of psychic experiences including prophetic dreams and encounters with ghosts, although only one of these – some menacing footsteps in a house elsewhere in Scotland – seems to have really frightened her. But it was her experience in a bedroom in Holyrood in 1890 which came a close second, judging from the details in a frank statement she provided to the Society for Psychical Research.

Lady Tweedale had a bedroom in the newer part of the palace but located close to some of the oldest rooms. One night she retired but, instead of going to sleep, began to read in bed under a bright light, 'alone in the room but not the least bit nervous'. The bed was a heavy iron model on coasters and had its head close against the wall. She stated: 'Suddenly I felt the bed shoved out from the wall, as if someone had taken the head and pulled it violently'.

Lady Tweedale looked round in amazement and again experienced the head being 'shoved away from the wall,' as she put it. 'I jumped up and saw that it had actually been moved – perhaps about a foot, so that there was a clear space between the head of the bed and the wall,

Left: *Mary, Queen of Scots on a contemporary coin.*

Below: *Holyrood Palace in the early nineteenth century.*

where there had not been before.' The incident was repeated the next night and thereafter Lady Tweedale took care never to be alone in the room again and the incident was never repeated.

What Lady Tweedale described as her 'sixth experience' of the psychic realm in her life also occurred in Holyrood. It took place around 1890 and involved seeing an apparition which, she wondered at the time, might have been Bothwell, the second husband of Mary Queen of Scots. The sighting came after a reception in Holyrood Palace which had been attended by around a thousand guests. The incident occurred late into the evening when most of the guests had departed and the ladies had congregated in a drawing room. The band was still playing and Lady Tweedale, who was somewhat fatigued, sat down to rest in a 'nook in the Throne Room'. The band were in sight and Lady Tweedale could also see a fastened door. This door was not merely locked, 'but one which had been fastened into the wall from some unknown date long ago'.

Suddenly her attention was caught by the sight of this hitherto immovable door swinging open and a man walking through. Lady Tweedale recalled initially that 'he was tall, dark, handsome, wore a military coat, all black – what I took to be the uniform of about Charles II's time'. In her frank account to Myers, Lady Tweedale regretted that she had not paid more attention to the uniform but she had seen so many people in uniform and court dress that evening that some uncertainty was understandable. Later in her statement she wondered if the figure could be dated to a more recent period. She closely observed the figure's behaviour and was astonished to see it walk straight through the middle of the band – she could not say whether it appeared to avoid band members or not – and then disappear through a centre window, which looked out upon a courtyard, some fifteen feet below.

Lady Tweedale immediately leapt up and asked the band master, 'Did you see anything?' to which he replied, 'No your Grace, but I felt a draft from that door,' pointing at the same time to the fastened door through which the figure had come.

On thinking about her experience, her Ladyship wondered if the figure resembled Bothwell but agreed that this was just an impression she had. However, she was sufficiently shaken by the experience at the time to report her sighting to the chaplain of Holyrood, Mr Hey Hunter. Later she was uncertain as to her identification of the figure as Bothwell, but on mentioning it to the psychical researcher Frederic Myers he took this impression sufficiently seriously and tried to find if it could in any way be confirmed. Unfortunately, it transpired that no portrait of Bothwell existed which would have settled the matter. Later what purported to be an artist's impression of Bothwell was obtained by a Scottish psychical researcher, Lord Bute. This was based upon a skeleton of a short, thick-set man found in Denmark and believed to be Bothwell. The hair where not white was reddish and the face was deformed by an injury to the eye socket. These physical characteristics seem to exclude Bothwell, and the identity of the apparition remains a mystery.

In the late 1970s the writer Joan Forman visited Holyrood for research for her book *Haunted Royal Homes* (1987). She heard stories of the Long Gallery being haunted by the sound of footsteps (heard by security staff) and by at least one apparition in the period 1976-77. One autumn day, a cleaner was at work at the top of a ladder by a window in the Long Gallery. The window was half opened and he saw framed within it, 'a human face wearing a stiff white ruff around its neck and a black coat, and a collar which was turned up'. He was so disturbed by his experience he quit work immediately and did not return, the contract ultimately being awarded to another window-cleaning company. For her own part Joan Forman encountered a strong sensation of a presence. She stated:

I found it quite impossible to stay in this, the small supper or supping room for more than a few minutes at a time, and matters were made worse by the fact that the sense of horror which

afflicts it appears to be concentrated in one single area, the left hand side near the entrance door. The sensation is so intense that it almost seems to have weight – as though the very air were thicker at that spot.

Although the room had been altered since the sixteenth century, Joan Forman identified it as the one in which Rizzio had been murdered, based upon contemporary descriptions of the killing. Some 140 years since the strange impressions felt by the Revd Dibdin, it seems that the room had lost none of its atmosphere.

Arthur's Seat

'The views from Arthur's Seat are preferable to dozing inside on a fine day, or using wine to stimulate wit…' said poet Robert Burns (1759-1796). The imposing hill of Arthur's Seat is all that remains of a small volcano which was last active, according to geologists, some 325 million years ago. The link with King Arthur is considered tenuous, but during the fifth century, Edinburgh and the surrounding area was the home to a short-lived kingdom called Rheged, which was comprised of refugees from other parts of Roman Britain. Traces of defensive ramparts and strip lynchetts may still be seen on the slopes but all other traces of the settlement and fortifications have vanished.

Arthur's Seat is associated with an intriguing mystery which remains unsolved to this day. In July 1836 some boys were searching for rabbit burrows and noticed some thin sheets of slate in the side of a cliff. Removing the slates they discovered a cave which was found to contain some

Opposite: *Holyrood Palace has been the scene of ghost sightings well into the twentieth century. (Photograph by Victoria Amador)*

Right: *The site of Rizzio's murder, where Joan Forman felt an intense atmosphere.*

seventeen tiny coffins, between three and four inches long. Each coffin contained a miniature wooden figure, each dressed differently in both style and material. The coffins were stacked in two tiers of eight with a third tier of one coffin. It was apparent that the coffins had been placed in the cave at intervals over many years, since a number showed signs of decay. The one on the top tier appeared to be quite recent, and others on the tier below were in a reasonable condition, but those on the bottom tier were rotting and the wrappings had disintegrated.

Of the seventeen specimens, only eight survived their initial discovery on account of the boys, 'pelting them at each other as unmeaning and contemptible trifles'. Once their burst of boyish energy was expended examples of the remainder were passed to more responsible hands, and to antiquaries.

The tiny coffins were detailed in the 1901-1902 *Proceedings of the Society of Antiquaries of Scotland*, (Vol. XXXII, p. 460) and several of the surviving specimens are contained in the Museum of Scotland in Queen Street, Edinburgh. One theory is that the coffins and the bodies represented a symbolic burial for the victims of the body snatchers Burke and Hare, or other resurrectionists who operated in the eighteenth and early nineteenth century. Certainly, there was great fear of body snatchers locally, for at Duddingstone village two kirk elders were assigned to watch over graves for three weeks after a body had been interred.

A writer for *The Scotsman* (16 July 1836) declared: 'Our own opinion would be – had we not some years ago abjured witchcraft and demonology – that there are still some of the weird sisters hovering around Mushat's Cairn or the Windy Growl who retain their ancient power to work the spells of death by entombing the likeness of those they wish to destroy'. The story reached the pages of *The Times* in London, but no explanation was ever forthcoming.

Arthur's Seat, early twentieth-century view by W.R. Reid.

The mystery has led to all kinds of curious and far-fetched speculation. The great collector of anomalies Charles Fort suggested – tongue in cheek – that the coffins might have been left as memorial by beings from another world. Equally whimsical was Harry Price in his book *Poltergeist Over England* (1945): speculating on why the coffins had been placed in the hill, rhetorically asking '…for what purpose? And by whom? Poltergeists or witches? The reader can decide for himself'. Another suggestion was that they were symbolic burials of sailors or fishermen lost at sea.

In Edinburgh for a folklore conference on 'Spirit Helpers' at the School of Scottish Studies at the end of October 2000, I was told by a delegate that there was a recent story of a ghostly black dog being seen on Arthur's Seat and that later the same apparition had appeared inside a nearby house.

The Sheep's Heid Inn

Although it appears modest from the outside, the Sheep's Heid Inn at Duddingstone has a fascinating interior which befits what is reputedly Scotland's oldest pub. Having narrowly escaped being converted into residential flats in recent years, the pub has been lovingly restored.

One unique feature is a skittle alley at the back of the pub, still used by a club whose members have been meeting at the inn since at least the last quarter of the nineteenth century. Appropriately as befits an ancient inn, the Sheep's Heid is haunted, with manifestations being reported into 2006.

The present building dates from the eighteenth century and, until the 1970s, had the distinction of being the only pub in Scotland where drinks were served outside. The Sheep's Heid gets its name from the soup once served here which consisted of boiled sheep's head (a favourite dish of witch-hunting King James I). Saved from closure in 2004, the interior of the Sheep's Heid has been lovingly restored by the current landlord and many old curios put back into the bar. With the restoration have come renewed reports of ghostly activity. The spirit of a little girl is said to haunt the skittle alley (according to a psychic who visited the inn with a BBC television crew in 2004). Like so many identifications by psychics, such claims are difficult to

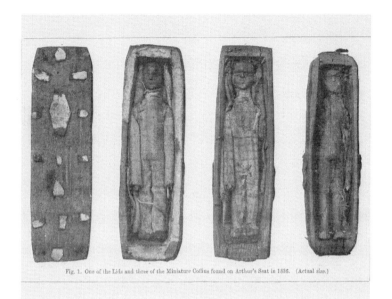

Fig. 1. One of the Lids and three of the Miniature Coffins found on Arthur's Seat in 1836. (Actual size.)

Specimens of the miniature coffins and effigies found on Arthur's Seat in 1836.

The haunted skittle alley in the Sheep's Heid Inn. (Photograph by Anna Pearce)

The Major's seat at the Sheep's Heid to which a former landlord returns. (Photograph by Anna Pearce)

corroborate in any way, but it must be said the area does have a strong atmosphere. Standing in the skittle alley, one is reminded of the classic description of a presence given by a butler named Sanders about Ballechin House, 'the most haunted house in Scotland', in 1897: '….a feeling that someone was present and about to speak to me.' (see *The Alleged Haunting of B----- House* (1900) by Ada Goodrich Freer and the Marquess of Bute).

In October 1993, it was reported that local taxi drivers passing the Sheep's Heid Inn had heard the clatter of skittles emanating from inside the ancient building. The noises were heard about 2.30 a.m., which falls within the peak time for many reports of ghost appearances.

Another interesting incident occurred early in 2006 when a young girl visiting the pub with her parents was seen to be apparently conducting an animated conversation with an invisible person occupying antique seating close to the bar. When asked as to the identity of her invisible friend, she replied firmly, 'the Old Major'. This caused some consternation to elderly regulars who recalled that the spot had been the favourite seat of a former landlord from the 1950s. He was a retired army major and known by all as 'the Major'.

From local recollections, it appears that in life the Major was famous for refusing to be disturbed if engrossed in one of his favourite parlour games at the table. His reluctance to stir extended to customers who might arrive whilst a game was in progress. All would have to wait until he had played his hand at cards or dominoes. An even longer wait could be in store if he was playing chess! Perhaps the Major is at the table still, but evidently prepared to welcome small child visitors…

FOUR

HAUNTED PLACES ABOVE
AND BELOW THE CITY

The Greyfriars Cemetery

Of all Edinburgh's haunted sites, the Greyfriars Cemetery has attracted the most publicity in recent years. For those intent upon a spooky experience, the Greyfriars churchyard undoubtedly meets the requirements with its atmospheric conditions best experienced on a night-time tour illuminated by a flickering candle flame… From the mid-1990s the Greyfriars Cemetery has been promoted as the most haunted cemetery in Great Britain, with the manifestations allegedly concentrated in the portion known as the Old Covenanters' Prison.

The Greyfriars Cemetery was originally given to the city by Mary Queen of Scots. Within it lies the Greyfriars church, famous as the place where the National Covenant was signed in 1638, seeking religious independence from the English Crown. The Covenant led to decades of sporadic rebellion and violence. Events came full circle when, forty-one years later, the survivors of the movement were captured after the Battle of Bothwell Bridge in 1679 and herded into iron cages in the south-west corner of the cemetery. Today one can still see the walled enclosure barred by an iron gate and labelled 'Covenanters' Prison'. Those who signed a bond for good behaviour in the future were released, whilst some 250 Covenanters who refused were sentenced to transportation to Barbados. However, the ship carrying them, ironically enough named *The Crown of London*, foundered on rocks off Orkney and all but fifty were drowned.

It must be said that the modern reputation that the Greyfriars Cemetery enjoys as a haunted place is rather a novelty in itself. Burial grounds in the British Isles appear relatively unhaunted, with the number of reliable ghost reports generated annually being virtually nil. This is a rather surprising fact, given how many grieving people visit cemeteries with thoughts of deceased loved ones at the forefront of their minds. However, as veteran British ghost hunter the late Andrew Green (1927-2004) often pointed out, ghosts invariably haunt places where people live, work and die, but not where their physical bodies are put to rest. As a result, the phantom most likely to be encountered in a graveyard would be the shade of a grave digger!

The image of Greyfriars as a place haunted by particularly pestilent spirits was first set in folklore in the nineteenth century. Local traditions held that a dark and gloomy set of tombs containing the remains of Sir George McKenzie Rosehaugh (1636-1691) were haunted. In life, McKenzie had been responsible for the prosecution and execution of many of the Covenanters (he boasted he had never lost a case for the King) and, after death, his uneasy spirit was held to haunt his mausoleum.

It became a dare for Edinburgh children to gather at the grill of the McKenzie tomb and chant:

Above and below *The historic Greyfriars church and graveyard. (Photographs by Anna Pearce)*

Bluidy Mackingie, come out if ye daur,
Lift the sneck, and draw the bar!

They would then immediately flee through the graveyard to avoid being seized by the dreaded ghost.

It seems that the reputation of the churchyard as a haunted place dwindled in the twentieth century. Other than being known as a particularly gloomy spot, little was heard about any psychic manifestations within its precincts and there seems to have been no hesitation for using 'Bluidy Mackingie's' mausoleum for the practical and mundane purpose of storing beds and bedding during an acute homelessness crisis in the city in the winter of 1945-1946.

Indeed, nothing was heard of any phantoms in the Greyfriars cemetery until the 1980s and the rise of popular ghost walks and tours in the city. It is an unwritten rule that a popular ghost walk should always include a cemetery, regardless of a lack of genuine apparitions. Greyfriars Cemetery was felt to be a perfect place for a tour and the rest is paranormal history. Such is the proliferation of claimed phenomena that there has ultimately been a book published, entitled *The Ghost That Haunted Itself – The Story of the McKenzie Poltergeist* (2001). Written by Jan-Andrew Henderson, the book is a work of what may be termed 'faction' – a dramatised telling of reportedly true events surrounding the 'City of the Dead Tour' which regularly took tourists through the cemetery and into the McKenzie tomb and the Covenanters' Prison. Statements from some of the 'victims' – many of whom were from outside the UK – are scattered through the text.

It seems local newspapers were more than happy to record the increasingly bizarre experiences claimed by participants on the tours. Visitors reported cold spots, feelings of nausea and mysterious cuts and bruises, seemingly the work of an invisible entity. Some twenty-nine people collapsed unconscious on the tour. According to published accounts, tour guides were alternatively amused, baffled and irritated by the turn of events and the failure of experts to shed any light on their ultimate nature. The alleged presence seems to have been dubbed a poltergeist because of the lack of reports of visible apparitions. Theoretical ideas about the nature of poltergeist phenomena were freely debated by the increasingly perplexed guides, who had to deal with participants fainting, or going into hysterics, during their cemetery tours.

Typical of the accounts was that of tourist Mandy Burgen from Cornwall, who wrote, 'In the tomb, I felt pain, just above my chest. After the tour, I unfastened my top and found a large red mark where the pain had been. I showed it to the others and, as they looked, three weals rose up in the same place. The next day they were gone.'

Ultimately, the guides became scared by their own experiences and the churchyard was closed for a period. Following this there was an outbreak of criminality, culminating in a seventeenth-century body being removed from a grave by two teenagers and mutilated. The culprits were convicted in March 2004 and were lucky to escape with suspended prison sentences.

Many people are convinced they have experienced something strange in the cemetery in recent years, but what is really going on? Whilst undoubtedly an atmospheric place, it should be noted that there was no tradition of haunting in the cemetery beyond a few suggestions in children's folklore prior to the 1990s. Even though it has been claimed that the story is '…one of the best documented and most conclusive paranormal cases in history', one need not go as far as the paranormal to explain the seizures and fainting spells.

It is noteworthy that in some rather reckless sources, Greyfriars Cemetery has been claimed as an inspiration for some of the nineteenth century's best-known supernatural stories. For instance, it has been claimed that in 1841 Charles Dickens misread the tombstone of a man called Scroggie, coming up with the name Scrooge for *A Christmas Carol*. It has also been claimed that

Above and below: *The Covenanters' Prison. (Photographs by Anna Pearce)*

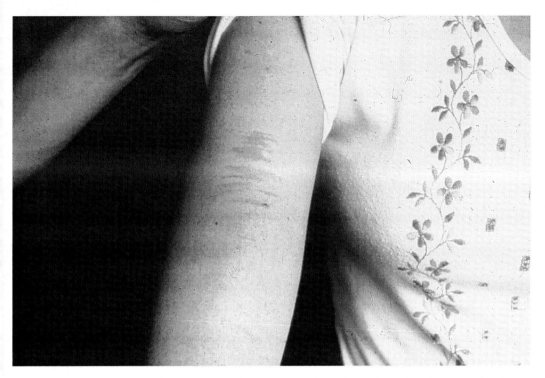

Alleged poltergeist scratches from a case in London in 1983. Similar marks and bruises have been reported in the McKenzie Vault by visitors. (Photograph by Andrew Green)

the two great authors of vampire fiction, John Polidori and Bram Stoker, visited the cemetery, but this is not supported by textual evidence in their works and many other locations have a better claim as potential inspiration or influence. Nonetheless, the alleged link with fictional creations may provide a clue to the mechanism behind at least some of the experiences.

Many of the symptoms reported by visitors at the Greyfriars Cemetery appear to have been generated by emotional excitement or hysteria leading to physical collapse. Such effects can be encountered when fictional supernatural dramas are performed. Fainting was a regular occurrence when the first stage version of *Dracula* was performed in the 1920s and 1930s, the effect enhanced by the suggestive presence of an actress dressed in a nurse's uniform tactfully standing at the stage door. These days such phenomena do not seem as common, perhaps because modern audiences are made of sterner stuff. In extreme cases, people have even been known to die of fright, but fortunately no fatality has occurred on any Edinburgh tour (doubtless an increase in numbers of tour participants would follow if one ever did!).

Hysteria seems to be at the root of many of the experiences claimed in the McKenzie Vault. More difficult to explain are the bruises and injuries, although there are all kinds of ways these might develop, particularly in a tightly packed group. It is possible that being physically present in the McKenzie Vault may trigger psychosomatic effects in particularly sensitive individuals. From the accounts in the book *The Ghost That Haunted Itself*, the quality of investigation at Greyfriars Cemetery did not rise to a particularly high level, despite the attentions of various mediums, psychics, and investigators drawn to the site, together with a large number of film makers, and broadcasters in search of a sensational story. Many seem to have accepted mundane events as

Right and below: *The atmosphere at Greyfriars Cemetery may have contributed to the sensations experienced within it. (Photographs by Anna Pearce and Philip Hutchinson)*

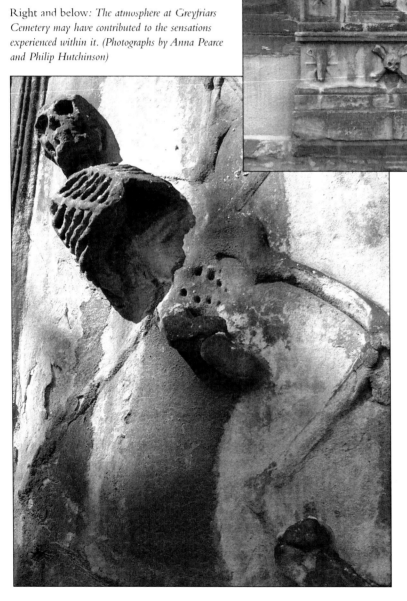

evidence of a psychic force at work. Although cases of poltergeists which supposedly inflict minor scratches or wounds on their victims have been occasionally reported, such cases are rare and are invariably linked with adolescents undergoing stress, where the possibility of self-harm or attention-seeking behaviour may arise.

It must also be said that the suggestibility of witnesses is a long-recognised problem in psychical research, whether ghost hunting or in séance room conditions. The problem can easily be demonstrated by getting any group of people in a dark room with a small light. If the audience is told the light is moving, a number of people will report seeing it change position, even if it is stationary.

Nonetheless, there remains the possibility that repeated visitors obsessed with ghosts may actually have triggered some kind of lingering psychic phenomena. Its origin might be the unconscious minds of visitors. Poltergeists are linked with living individuals undergoing stress, and occasionally groups of people imitating séance conditions have succeeded in creating apparently psychokinetic phenomena in the form of raps and object movements. The most famous example was the 'Philip' group based in Toronto in the early 1970s, who invented an artificial ghost called Philip, and succeeded in obtaining rapping sounds and the strange movement of a table. However, the 'ghost' was a product of their unconscious minds, and ceased its activities when the group disbanded. It is conceivable that concentrating on an imaginary entity called the McKenzie poltergeist has actually succeeded in creating psychokinetic effects, although the source is the unconscious minds of the participants, rather than an external entity. Thus, the name of 'the ghost that haunted itself', might well be an accurate reflection of the situation…

The South Bridge Vaults

Second only to the Greyfriars Cemetery as a centre of alleged psychic activity are the South Bridge Vaults. Although the alleged phenomena are not as dramatic as those in the Greyfriars Cemetery, since 1994 mediums, psychical researchers, ghost-tour guides, latter-day witches, and numerous visitors, have all claimed their share of strange experiences down in these eighteenth-century chambers.

Sightings of an apparition of a gentleman in eighteenth-century clothes, nicknamed 'the Watcher', have occurred, though many more claim to have felt this presence, rather than seen him. In June 1995 there were repeated reports of strange lights being seen in the Vaults, and in May 1996 came the sighting of the ghost of an old woman. Other stories maintain the Vaults were said to be haunted by a boy who pulls at clothing, and by another more malign entity nicknamed 'Mr Boots', who allegedly pushes people, and whispers obscenities, but does not seem to be as vicious or unpleasant as the alleged McKenzie poltergeist at Greyfriars. A lengthy list of what were claimed to be psychic incidents over 1994-1996 was compiled for a book on underground Edinburgh and, according to a dossier compiled by Mercat Tours over the last decades, suggests the invisible presence also haunts a bar known as 'Whistle Binkies' on Niddry Street.

On account of their reputation, the South Bridge Vaults in Edinburgh were selected in 2003 for a series of ghost-hunting experiments conducted by Dr Richard Wiseman of the University of Hertford, to record the reactions of people in supposedly haunted places. Some 250 volunteers took part in the tests, and the results were published in May 2003 in the *British Journal of Psychology*.

As with the Vaults at Edinburgh Castle and the McKenzie Mausoleum, going down into these subterranean chambers when lit only by small candles and lanterns, can certainly prove an eerie experience. Findings suggested that a substantial number of people were prone to interpret areas with naturally occurring cold spots, poor lighting, and strong magnetic fields, as haunted

The Vaults, scene of many ghost hunts.
(Photographs by Philip Hutchinson)

Whistle Binkies bar along Niddry Street, said to be haunted by an entity coming up from the Vaults.

locations. A further problem – often found with séance room investigations – is that witnesses may become highly suggestible in the dark. Some participants reported strong feelings of anxiety, but little in the way of visual apparitions were recorded. Dr Wiseman postulated that ghost experiences might be a form of warning, triggered by a person's subconscious mind responding to slight sensory perceptions, which indicate possible dangerous or claustrophobic situations. With the added effects of suggestion, this theory may also explain many complaints of distressing sensations and hysteria on the part of visitors as in the Greyfriars Cemetery. Whilst confirming that people may feel uneasy in spooky locations, the theory fails to address the fact that ghosts can be encountered in mundane settings, such as ordinary houses or offices as well as in more romantic and dramatic locations, such as stately homes or castle dungeons.

The Vaults have also featured as a site for photographic anomalies, particularly so-called orbs which appear as circular spots of light on prints taken with digital cameras. Since orbs were first reported in the early 1990s, there have been many who have claimed (or wished) the phenomena to be taken as proof of psychic activity, but there is no good reason to identify them as such, given the existence of perfectly normal explanations. The air is constantly filled with minute specks of moisture, smoke, or dust, and these may be recorded on sensitive cameras, particularly where the flash is situated close to the lens, as with most modern cameras. That 'orbs' should show up in dusty locations such as the Vaults, is entirely predictable. More difficult to explain are the persistent failures of electrical equipment. There were also repeated reports of torch and flashlight failures, as though batteries had been drained. Nonetheless, there is an uncertainty with some photographs showing fogging and misting effects, which may indicate the presence of electromagnetic energy of some kind.

Reports of phenomena in the Vaults also led to investigations by the Ghost Club and others in 2003. Odd noises were also heard in the night, including one which 'I can only describe as a heel dragging on the floor'. Other odd sounds heard during the night have included a sawing sound, banging sounds, and a sigh. Unfortunately, a large underground space with adjacent derelict buildings is a difficult site to explore, and exclude ordinary sounds from, and the causes may be difficult to pin down. Ultimately, more research will be needed to determine conclusively the cause of the experiences reported in the Vaults.

George Street and Princes Street

The popular ghost book writer Elliot O'Donnell (1873-1965) claimed that a gentleman friend had seen the ghost of a woman in white, early in the twentieth century, in George Street. The apparition was also supposedly seen by a policeman and others. It was said to be that of a Miss Jane Vernelt, who had ran a costumier's business in George Street in 1892, and died in an insane asylum after parting with her business. Thereafter, her ghost was seen gliding along George Street and disappearing into the chemist's shop which occupied the site of her former business. The clothes and appearance of 'Jane of George Street' are given in exhaustive detail, describing her as 'a strikingly fair woman with very pale yellow hair…[and]…a startlingly white complexion' which at close quarters resembled 'the face of the dead'. A woman who allegedly knew the background to much of the story, was a Miss Bosworth who had lived in St Michael's Road, Bournemouth during the First World War.

Despite these circumstantial details, it must be said that Elliot O'Donnell was often an unreliable writer, whose life-long absorption in ghost stories seems to have weakened his critical faculties, and on occasion prompted him into sheer invention, or to the recycling of old stories with new locations. Entertainingly shuddersome as his story may be, little reliance can be placed on his tale unless any of the information can be corroborated.

Running parallel with George Street is Princes Street, the retailing centre of Edinburgh. During the nineteenth century the journalist and spiritualist W.T. Stead recorded an account of a crisis apparition at a property on Princes Street. However, by their very nature crisis apparitions are one-off events, and so there would be no returning presence. However, veteran ghost hunter Andrew Green (1927-2004) discovered that the apparition of a gentleman in a tall black hat with a walking cane had been seen in Princes Street in previous years, 'walking slowly and rather sedately' towards Charlotte Street. The last recorded sighting seems to have been in 1975.

Edinburgh Evening News Building, North Bridge

Journalist and ghost hunter the late James Wentworth Day (1899-1983) once observed that newspapermen and press photographers are a sceptical bunch who believed in expense accounts and good living and are, likely as not, to treat ghost stories with amusement or scorn. Today his view is perhaps best described as a caricature, for scattered throughout Great Britain there are stories of haunted newspaper offices, and the large offices of the *Edinburgh Evening News* may be the most haunted of all with possibly as many as three ghosts.

The most detailed sighting occurred on the evening of Monday 14 November 1994 when Scott McKirdy, a page compiler and paste-up artist with the paper saw the ghost of a man striding 'purposefully' along a basement corridor. His attention at the scene had initially been caught

George Street in the nineteenth century.

by a door in the basement, which he had previously never noticed in his time in the thirteen-storey building. Then he spotted the figure:

> He was wearing matching brown trousers and jersey and was wearing a blue apron tied at the back. In his arms he had a big wooden tray filled with bits of metal the size of match boxes and it looked really heavy... He didn't look like a shadow at all.

The figure made no sound at all, and realising that he was witnessing an apparition, Mr McKirdy found himself gripped by fear. He stated, 'I don't know why but my body just took over.'

On checking the basement where the figure had appeared colleagues found a door, but it had apparently been locked for at least a month. Scott McKirdy recalled that he had heard no sound such as fumbling for keys, or the noise of any door being opened. Understandably excited about having a ghost on its premises, the paper ran a headline: 'Printer from the grave spooks worker at News'. In the course of enquiries they learned of at least two other hauntings associated with their offices, which had been built in 1905.

Front of counter staff reported a ghost which brushed past them. 'The female spirit, who always dressed in black, appears to walk towards the staff entrance' was the description given in the paper, eagerly covering its own haunting. In yet another case a security guard was said to have been greatly alarmed by seeing a former colleague who died in 1990.

Further comments on the alleged presence in the building came from Inez Hamilton, a clairvoyant from Stockbridge, who said there was 'no doubt that he saw a spirit... there were very strong spiritual vibrations down in the area.' Ms Hamilton maintained that the ghost was the spirit of a printer, who had loved his job so much that he returned after death, and that she also felt 'there's more than just one person still working down there.'

However, alternative theories to unquiet spirits were put forward by Alex Wallace from the Scottish Society for Psychical Research, and another medium. They speculated that Scott's work in the paste-up room constructing pages, had momentarily formed a mental link with a former printer or typesetter who constructed pages in the past, resulting in the appearance of an apparition. Concerns for the staff – and the instinct for a good story – led to the newspaper to call in a medium named Tina Wylie, who also suggested that Scott had experienced what she described as a 'time warp', a crossover between time dimensions.

Investigation of the history of the site revealed that it stood on what was once Cape and Feather Close, another part of old underground Edinburgh which had been sealed up after a visitation by the plague. Historians also revealed that the Close had been the home of an eighteenth-century poet, Robert Fergusson, who had died in the Bedlam insane asylum at the age of twenty-three, but all the indicators are that the haunting presences in the building are of a much more modern origin.

Haunted Theatres

Many old theatres can claim ghosts, and Edinburgh has at least two examples among the city's theatre district, which lies to the West of the Castle Hill, between the Grassmarket and Lothian Road.

The building which housed the old Empire Theatre burned down in 1911, with some nine people dying in the fire. The theatre was re-established in the 1990s as the Festival Theatre, and a number of strange incidents, including apparitions, have been reported since.

Among the victims of the 1911 blaze was the skilled conjuror and illusionist Lafayette, who was cremated and buried in Piershill Cemetery after an initial mix-up over the identity of his body. There is much speculation that a tall, dark, shadowy figure seen in the Festival Theatre since 1995, may be the great Lafayette making a return. The figure has been seen in the circle area of the auditorium and also on the stage. Mysterious cold spots have also been encountered by staff.

Ghosts also haunt the Lyceum Theatre, built in 1883. The Lyceum has a fine Victorian interior, and was beautifully remodelled in 1992 with a glass foyer. Ghostly laughter has been reported coming from the auditorium after performances are over, and occasionally during play rehearsals. A woman in blue has also been seen in the upper gallery, which is not normally open to the public during performances.

FIVE

HAUNTED HOUSES
GREAT AND SMALL

Charlotte Square

During the 1960s, Charlotte Square and the adjacent Charlotte Street gained a reputation for being haunted by no less than four ghosts, and attracting large numbers of American students of psychic phenomena as a result. The reasons are now hard to grasp, but the late Andrew Green recorded several of these apparitions in his study *Ghosts of Today* (1980), maintaining that a phantom coach appears outside a certain house in the Square, but vanishes when someone approaches it. Another story has the Square haunted by the ghostly form of a female beggar.

This apparition must be different to the other recorded by Andrew Green, of a woman in eighteenth-century costume walking up the road to the Square, and fading away just as she turns left. According to witnesses, she was described as 'well dressed and gave the impression of being "quality".' However, another story maintains that the ghost beggar is actually male, perhaps one of a tribe of street children found in the city in the eighteenth and nineteenth centuries. One visitor described them as 'a very useful kind of blackguard called Cawdys, who attend at taverns, coffee houses and other public places, to go on errands… These boys though in rags lie every night upon the stairs, or in the streets, are yet considerably trusted, and have seldom proved unfaithful.' Confusingly, some stories have the beggar as a mournful-looking old man, whilst other stories speak of a hooded figure like a monk completing the Square's contingent of spectres.

Blackett Place

What was certainly one of the best-documented haunted houses in Victorian Edinburgh, stands a short distance along Blackett Place. Details were collected in 1885 by a Mrs Brietzcke, an associate of the Society for Psychical Research. The precise identity of the house, and the name of the family who had occupied it from 1871, were concealed at the time. The Society was impressed with the testimony and published details in its journal in July 1886. Members of the household repeatedly saw the figure of a woman in white. Like many ghosts it seemed to have a tendency for manifesting on the staircase, and there was a second male presence which appeared in a downstairs room. The first to see the ghost was one of the daughters of the house, one autumn afternoon, about 4 p.m. She stated:

I saw the figure of a woman, above the medium size, standing on about the fourth step from the bottom; she had her arms folded, and was draped all over (head included) in white; she seemed to be

watching me… the thrill that ran through me made me fly into the schoolroom; but almost immediately after I ran out again to see if it was only a fancy; and found it had disappeared.

The girl never mentioned the figure to her mother, or to anyone else, and felt rather ashamed of her fear, but the same apparition went to on to appear to almost everyone in the house.

Another daughter had a similar encounter on the staircase. Whilst ascending the stairs, she looked up to see the tall, white figure of a woman on the landing above. She could see the form distinctly, but could see right through it. She recalled, 'It looked at me for a few seconds, then turned and walked into the passage, leading to the bathroom. Not knowing what it was, I had not the slightest fear, and I followed it there. Of course, when I got there the room was empty.'

The usual place for the ghost to appear was upon the staircase or landing, but on one occasion it manifested in the mother's room. The daughter who saw it stated, '…it stood with arms folded, looking straight at me, with a most heart-broken expression in the eyes. Even at first glance it did not look real, as the dark blue curtain was visible all through it, but less so at the face and shoulders.' The face appeared sad and sweet, and the girl did not feel frightened, and approached only to find nothing before or behind the curtain. At that point she felt afraid and fled the room.

Whilst these appearances were harmless, it seems that the manifestations could take on a malevolent character on occasion, with the ghost being blamed for several accidents. On a particular evening, one of the three daughters went upstairs to a store room to fetch some wine (they did not use the basement because of damp). Suddenly there came a crash, and another sister

Right: *Sinister apparitions were recorded in a house on Blackett Place in the Victorian era. (Illustration by Edie Rogers)*

Opposite: *Charlotte Square gained a reputation as a centre of ghostly activity in the 1960s.*

came running out in alarm. She found her sister lying unconscious at the bottom of the stairs, surrounded by broken bottles. As she looked at the scene, she noticed the same female figure in white standing at the bend of the staircase. Her immediate thought was that her sister had fainted on seeing the ghost, but when she came to, she said she had not seen anything but had felt a sharp blow on her back which had sent her tumbling, but she 'had fallen so marvellously that she had not hurt herself.' Physical manifestations, and sensations of being touched, were also reported at other times, and one informant recorded, 'We often had our heads touched, and in my case I used to feel all five fingers distinctly.'

Another serious incident occurred when the family cook was badly scared by the ghost appearing on the stairs. The cook was carrying hot water bottles at the time, and in her fright did not notice that a bottle had slipped. On fleeing downstairs she found she had burned her arm severely.

The apparition of the woman in white may not have been the only presence in the house. On a particular evening, one of the daughters was sitting alone in the dining room. The rest of the household were out at a concert, with the exception of the smallest child, who was in bed. The girl was working in the dining room (she does not say what at) when a feeling came over her that she was not alone in the room, and that she was being watched. She recalled, 'Looking up, and just appearing around the door [of a cupboard] was the face of a man, the most wicked and evil-looking face I have ever seen, more like a demon's face than anything else. The skin was a yellowy colour, and it had black hair, moustache and beard.' Its eyes were fixed upon her,

Phenomena at Trinity fit the pattern of poltergeist disturbances although the word was not in use at the time.

and more of the head stretched around the door, exposing the neck. The face continued to regard her until she began to collect her senses and thought, 'That can't be a ghost, for it isn't transparent like the others.' She continued to stare at it for what she estimated as a quarter of an hour until the head withdrew. She still sat there petrified, expecting it to return. When the rest of the household returned they looked in the cupboard and found nothing but shelves, 'it was an impossibility for anybody to get into it'.

Strange noises were also heard in the property. Initially, these were blamed upon rats, but they were all puzzled by a particularly loud thump, or booming noise, heard in various parts of the house. This occurred so regularly that it became known as the 'morning bang' (the key time was 6 a.m.) but its cause was never found. Sounds like pacing steps were also heard and, one night the cook and a housemaid heard a rustling sound around 1 a.m. from different parts of the house. The cook described it as 'a lot of dead leaves like'. But one phenomenon which certainly could not be explained by rats was the experience of members of the family hearing their names distinctly being called from the dining room. On going into the room it was always empty.

The ghost was eventually linked with the suicide of a married woman in the bathroom of the house.

Trinity

It is rare for a ghost to result in legal proceedings – but not unknown. In 1998 a cottage in Derbyshire was the subject of litigation on the part of purchasers, who wished to sue the vendors for having sold them a property with ghosts (the claim was dismissed). However, a case of what Victorian ghost book writers described as 'one of the most curious law suits of recent years' concerned a dwelling house at Trinity, near the Newhaven Harbour, in 1835. The litigation took some two years, and was never satisfactorily resolved.

Maurice Lothian, who became procurator fiscal, left a detailed account of the strange proceedings. He was employed by the plaintiff, a Captain Molesworth, who had rented the house of a Mr Webster (who lived in an adjoining property). In May or June 1836 the Molesworth family began to experience extraordinary noises, which were impossible to explain. Captain Molesworth concluded that they must have been the work of Mr Webster, who strongly rejected the allegations, maintaining there was no reason why he should seek to damage the reputation of his property.

Studying the case it appears that the ghost was heard rather than seen, but it created a wide variety of sounds, both day and night, 'footsteps of invisible feet, knockings, scratchings, and rustlings, first on one side then on another'. The knocks on occasions seemed to resemble a tune, suggesting some kind of intelligence was at work. Efforts were made at communication, and it was found that the noises could respond numerically to questions such as 'How many people are there in this room?' by rapping out the correct number. The walls were seen to tremble visibly, but no physical person could be found concealed behind them.

The events occurred too early to be dubbed a poltergeist, for it was not until 1848 that the Edinburgh writer Mrs Catherine Crowe introduced the word into English from the German language. Captain Molesworth had recently lost a daughter called Matilda, and local people began to attribute the manifestations to her agency from beyond the grave, and uttered dire warnings that her sickly thirteen-year-old sister Jane would soon follow her. For his part, Mr Webster had no hesitation in accusing the living sister of causing all the disturbances.

Jane did not survive for long. In his crusade against his presumed trickster, Captain

Molesworth recruited officers from his regiment in Leith, together with masons, justices of the peace, and sheriff's officers in an attempt to catch or frighten away the tormentor. A cordon was formed around the house, but to no avail, and in another experiment Jane was restrained by being tied up in a bag. This did nothing to stem the fusillade of raps and knocks. Jane's health declined further, and she died as a result, it was declared, 'of the severe measures to which she was subjected'.

Depressed, ill and at a loss, Captain Molesworth quit the house with his family, and after their departure the manifestations ceased. Today, what makes the case convincing is the similarity with many other cases of its type worldwide.

15 Learmonth Gardens – Sir Alexander Seton and the Cursed Bone

What would undoubtedly count as one of the oldest ghosts to have ever manifested in Edinburgh was that which reputedly invaded the household of Sir Alexander Seton at 15 Learmonth Gardens in the mid-1930s. This was not a ghost dating from the sixteenth or seventeenth century but a far older presence, dating to before the birth of Christ, for Sir Alexander Seton and his wife believed themselves to be haunted by a 3,000 year-old spirit from ancient Egypt.

'I went in to get some cigarettes, and, on opening the door, I found to my amazement that the glass case and bone were completely shattered.' So begins one of Sir Alexander Seton's many accounts of the dramatic poltergeist incidents which occurred in his Edinburgh home, and were linked with his possession of an ancient bone that his wife, Lady Zeyla, had taken from a tomb in Egypt.

The tale is very much a story of its time, an era when wealthy, titled individuals like the Setons could still dabble in Egyptology, and bring home relics with little practical restriction upon them. The discovery of Tutankhamen's tomb in 1922 had generated a public fever for ancient Egypt, which had still not subsided over a decade later, when Sir Alexander Seton and his wife Lady Zeyla took a holiday in Egypt in 1936. During the course of a visit to some ancient tombs, the couple looked down into a pit, and saw it was filled with skeletal remains. Lady Zeyla expressed a desire to obtain a relic and, after a great deal of coaxing, managed to persuade an Egyptian man to crawl into the pit and obtain a bone for her. It was a sacrum bone from the lower part of the spine. The couple 'treated it as a joke', but a native Egyptian implored Lady Zeyla not to take it away but to leave it where it was, or replace it. Lady Zeyla did neither, and the bone returned to Scotland with the couple as a souvenir of their visit.

The Setons soon regretted their sacrilege. On their return to Learmonth Gardens, poltergeist phenomena broke out in the house with the smashing of ornaments, including a glass flower vase. In an account given to News Chronicle, Sir Alexander stated: 'I have no explanations. I can offer no reasons for these happenings. I would like to emphasise to critics that I am not a frightened housewife, and I am not in the habit of breaking up my own glassware in my own house.'

In February 1937 Sir Alexander's nine-year-old nephew came and stayed in the house. He knew nothing of the bone, or the strange stories which had been in circulation. But he was puzzled to see a curious, robed figure striding through the house. When the bone was lent to a surgeon friend of Sir Alexander, a similar phantom was witnessed in the surgeon's house by a maid. She was so terrified that she ran from the figure, and broke her leg in the process of trying to flee.

On the return of the bone to the Seton household the disturbances continued. Sounds of someone moving through the house were heard, and furniture was moved and broken. During a dinner party the table on which the bone was placed moved by itself, terrifying guests, and later a glass display case which housed the relic was overturned and smashed.

Right: *Lady Zeyla with the 'cursed' Egyptian bone.*

Below: *The story of the 'cursed' bone caused a sensation in the 1930s.*

THE STRANGE STORY OF MY HAUNTED HOUSE

tomb itself. On the top of it lay a beautiful alabaster headrest. There was a lot of jewellery turned black with age.

Around the tomb were the bones of slaughtered animals. There were bronze needles lying

Different reports have appeared about the uncanny happenings in the Edinburgh house of Sir ALEXANDER SETON. News Chronicle asked him to tell his own story, giving the truth about the queer affair. He sat down and wrote this story :—

heard him crying. He came up to the top landing, where my

dread of knowing one was not alone.

to make arrangements with our only maid about tea, but, as she

Sir Alexander gave a talk about the disturbances to the Edinburgh Psychic College in April 1937. The meeting was packed and a number of psychics and mediums – very much in vogue in the 1930s – were attracted by the sensational publicity. A number suggested that the Setons would have to rid themselves of the bone once and for all, and individuals came forward, volunteering to take the relic back to Egypt. The intense interest of newspapers across the English-speaking world was perhaps predictable. Cinema audiences were being thrilled and horrified by 'Mummy' pictures from Hollywood's Universal Studios, (author Sir John Mortimer recalled witnessing his tough public-school boxing instructor collapse in fright in one such film). It seems many were more than happy to believe the Curse of the Pharaohs had reached all the way to Scotland, and was striking the aristocracy. In contrast to the publicity of the alleged Curse of Tutankhamen in 1923, when people desperately sought to dispose of Egyptian relics by sending them to the British Museum, over eighty people came forward offering to acquire the bone from the Setons. Among these were the Society for Psychical Research, who on 8 April 1937 offered to take custody of the bone, but this did not happen.

The stories gained ever-wider circulation with the *Los Angeles Times* running headlines such as 'Bone starts ghosts wandering Scots send it back to Tomb'. Eventually, without consulting his wife, Sir Alexander had the bone exorcised by an uncle, who was in holy orders at Fort Augustus, and he then burned the relic to ashes in a solemn ceremony. For the Setons, the publicity had provided a screen and diversion from their increasingly troubled domestic life. Within a few years they were divorced, and to some extent the story of the cursed bone may have provided an excuse for the failure of their marital relationship and other troubles.

At least one writer, Ian Wilson, has proposed that this was the whole solution to the tale of the cursed bone. However, it is possible that the reality may be more complex. There is no doubt that the Seton household was a stressful one. Stress is a feature in poltergeist cases worldwide, and although poltergeists are often associated with adolescents, in more recent years it has been recognised that adults may also be the focus for these phenomena. Could Lady Zeyla herself have been the origin of the disturbances, either causing the damage in fits of hysteria, or in an attempt to get attention?

Where an object becomes a focus of superstitious or symbolic dread, it may be able to induce a subconscious reaction, which, in turn, can manifest as a poltergeist manifestation. Sir Alexander kept a diary of the disturbances; throughout he referred repeatedly to it as 'the Bone'. It is possible that there were genuine psychic manifestations occurring in the Seton household, but that their origins lay in the tensions in the subconscious minds of the occupants.

The story of the cursed Egyptian bone of Learmonth Gardens is also notable as the last of its type. After the Second World War, the study of ancient Egypt became a specialist field, controlled by professional archaeologists, museum curators, and university scholars. With amateur access to relics and excavations now denied, allegedly 'true' stories of curses and hauntings linked with Egyptian artefacts have vanished completely from the psychic scene.

In contrast, poltergeist-type events show no sign of diminution. Not far from the site of Sir Alexander's former home, standing in the middle of Learmonth Terrace, is the Learmonth Hotel. It has been troubled by a poltergeist-like entity for the past twenty-five years. The speciality of the presence is opening and closing doors – much to the annoyance of night porters – even if the doors have been locked. Footsteps disturbed staff in the 1980s, along with the curious sound of whistling heard coming from the conference room. Whenever the room was checked it was always found to be empty. Odd electrical activity – as with so many haunted properties – has also been cited as taking place, taking the more novel form of hairdryers switching themselves on and off inside rooms.

The Learmonth Hotel, home to a poltergeist.

Craigcrook Castle. (Photograph by Victoria Amador)

Craigcrook Castle

'Ghost Returns to Judge's Old Haunt' was the claim made regarding the sixteenth-century Craigcrook Castle in the *Daily Record* in July 1970. Standing on Edinburgh's Corstorphine Hill, the building gained a reputation for being haunted at the end of the 1960s, when it underwent alteration for occupation, by a firm of architects, Alison & Hutchinson.

The first reports of phenomena at Craigcrook Castle came in 1969, when an accountant named Charles Cameron conducted two all-night vigils in the castle on successive nights. He was rewarded by hearing footsteps outside the Jeffreys' library, together with a shuffling, 'as if cloth or a heavy object was being dragged across the floor'. As in so many accounts of footsteps, the noises seemed curiously shy about entering the room where the listener was actually stationed, almost as though the human eye deters such activity. A similar pattern has been noticed in poltergeist incidents where objects may be encountered in mid-flight, but are rarely seen to start to move. Sensations of an intense cold were also experienced in the library, and on one occasion the doorbell rang when there was no one present.

In June 1970 staff working at the building began complaining of flying paper clips. At first it was all taken as a joke, but one which rapidly soured after one of the female workers was cut by a pin and another was struck by a two-inch screw. Catherine Johnson, a seventeen-year-old office junior, stated: 'At first it was more annoying than frightening, but then we realised it couldn't have been someone playing jokes... Several of us were struck at one time or another... and clips and things weren't going slowly.'

Mr Ronald Adamson, a fifty-six-year-old librarian who lived at Craiglockhart Grove, said 'I was terribly sceptical then a paper clip landed on the desk one day. I was looking for it when something shot straight past me from the desk. How could anyone engineer that?' Cold spots were also experienced, and again the doorbell rang by itself. As a result, a senior partner of the firm called in a priest to conduct an exorcism in a bid to bring the haunting to an end, amid newspaper suggestions that the haunting entity or entities were the souls of victims of the ruthless seventeenth-century Judge Jeffreys, or even 'the tortured soul of Jeffreys himself'.

The attribution of victims of Judge Jeffreys as the cause of the phenomena seems to have arisen from journalistic licence. Leaving aside questions of why condemned prisoners, or the judge, from the seventeenth century should manifest there, the confusion seems to have arisen with the eighteenth-century Lord Jeffrey to whom the library was dedicated. Altogether more informed writers have claimed the spirit as the later Lord Jeffrey, who found an infamous literary immortality with the opening sentence in his review of Wordsworth's *Excursion*: 'This will never do'.

Alternative local candidates for the identity of the ghosts include a murdered woman called Helen Hall, or Helen Bell, who worked as a housekeeper at the building in the eighteenth century. The owner of the house was a man named Strachan, who also kept a house in High Street. During his absence, Helen was murdered by two men who later stood trial for her killing, but escaped conviction. Her vexed spirit is still said to walk, seeking justice.

However, unlikely as it seems, the practice of nicknaming a poltergeist 'Jeff' or 'Jeffrey' is not without precedent, and indeed seems well-established in folklore. Examples include 'Jeff' at Epworth Parsonage, Lincolnshire in 1716, 'Old Jeffrey' at Willington Mill on Tyneside in the early nineteenth century, and Gef, the infamous 'talking mongoose poltergeist' which supposedly manifested in a farmhouse on the Isle of Man in 1936.

Grange House (Now Demolished)

At the time of its demolition in March 1936 the Grange House, which stood close to Grange Cemetery, off Lover's Loan, looked every part the haunted mansion. Grange House was built upon the site of the monastic Grange of St Giles – legend held that the monks built a secret tunnel running to the Kirk of St Giles. The property served as the pre-Reformation home of the vicars of St Giles until becoming a private house. Originally a single tower with one chimney, it was acquired by the Cant family, who added further towers and turrets. The property passed to the Dicks of Braid in 1631, in a bargain made on a golf course; they continued adding to the building over the generations.

By the time they had finished the Gothic decorations, including menacing statues of gryphons on the gates, the Grange looked every bit the archetypal haunted house. It was later acquired by the Pelham-Burns family. Later in the nineteenth century it was used as a school for young ladies. Like many ancient Scottish homes and family seats, the building was said to be frequented by a ghostly Green Lady. An old mirror hanging in the building was credited with showing figures to some who gazed into it, which were not physically present in the room. The extensive grounds were also said to be haunted, containing on the north side a path known as the Monk's Walk which ran to a 'monk's seat'. Around this seat hovered – although apparently never sitting upon the seat itself – a cowled monastic figure with a terribly bruised face.

The ghosts were heard rather than seen. Within Grange House, the spirit of an old miser was said to roll a (presumably spectral) barrel of coins down a corridor. This may have been a legend

Opposite: *A house on Garscube Terrace was haunted by a suicide's ghost in the mid-1950s.*

Left: *The infamous Judge Jeffreys has been proposed as the entity haunting Craigcrook Castle but seems an unlikely candidate.*

to account for the strange noises which were heard in the house in the nineteenth century, most notably by a Miss Dick-Lauder, a member of the family who stayed periodically at Grange House. On one occasion, the house being filled with visitors, Miss Dick-Lauder had to sleep in a bedroom known as Lady Lauder's Boudoir. During the early hours of the morning (a peak time, it may be noted, for ghostly experiences) she awoke to hear a curious rumbling sound. The noises increased and stopped exactly opposite her door. The young woman expected to see the door open but nothing happened. Then much to her relief, the sounds ceased, and she sprang out of bed and locked her door. But as she returned to bed the strange sounds recommenced, again approaching and stopping right outside her door. In a state of near hysteria she lay in bed, trembling in fearful anticipation. The sounds recommenced a third time, increasing gradually – when she heard footsteps stopping at her door, Miss Dick-Lauder fainted with fright.

On reviving she lay motionless in bed, but was relieved to hear no further noises. With the arrival of dawn she rose immediately, and dressed in haste, intending to leave by a coach which left the Grassmarket at 6 a.m. On making her farewells she resolved to tell no one about her experience, although she later narrated the events of the night to her sister.

However, a few weeks later the young lady was again staying at the Grange, and was present at dinner when a retired colonel asked Sir Thomas if the house was haunted. Members of the family recounted the traditional ghost stories, including one from Mrs Stark, the third daughter of Sir Alexander Dick. In the course of these tales it was noted that Miss Dick-Lauder had

turned very pale, and on enquiry being made she admitted frankly to the experiences which had deeply shaken her. It was then revealed that many strangers staying at the Grange had heard the same sound, which was compared to heavy luggage being hauled across the floor.

Despite the frequent nature of these occurrences, no explanation was ever discovered, and the strange incidents were destined to remain forever a mystery after Grange House was demolished in the spring of 1936.

Garscube Terrace

It is a fact that most ghosts appear when they are least expected, and a good example of one such manifestation occurred in 1955 at an early Victorian House on Garscube Terrace, to the north-west of the city. Alan Bogue, a nineteen-year-old apprentice painter, was working on cleaning down a fourth-storey bathroom floor when he heard footsteps behind him. Initially he thought there was nothing unusual about this, as his workmate was also on the premises. Just as he moved into the entrance of the door the footsteps seemed to reach him; simultaneously he was struck by what seemed like an electric shock, accompanied by a flash of light. Startled and dazzled, he tottered to his feet, and staggered towards a bedroom, to sit down for a moment to recover. As he did so the bedroom door opened by itself, although he did not absorb the significance of this at the time.

On recovering he gingerly approached the bathroom again, only to experience a second, less powerful, shock, followed by an overwhelming feeling of grief, bringing him close to tears. At this point his workmate Bill Oliver arrived on the scene. Bill's reaction was marked – his face was drained of colour and he staggered back from Alan Bogue. Then he suddenly seemed to go into a frenzy and he launched himself into a physical assault upon Alan. Fortunately, this insane fit was a temporary seizure – Bill suddenly regained control of himself and profusely apologised. As Alan Brogue attempted to make sense of the incident, Bill then revealed he had been told by the owner of the flat that the need for redecoration had arisen from the suicide of the previous tenant. A young school teacher, Anne B., had hanged herself with a dressing-gown cord following the breaking off of her engagement by her fiancé.

Neither man saw anything through the remainder of their work – it says much for their fortitude that they were prepared to continue – but the feeling of sadness persisted throughout their time on the premises. Understandably Alan Bogue's experience stayed with him and impressed him sufficiently to inform Peter Moss, who collected true ghost experiences in the early 1970s and later published them in *Ghosts Over Britain* (1976).

Such experiences of a seemingly electrical nature are not unknown; as will be noticed in this book a number of haunted properties suffer from electrical anomalies. The veteran journalist and founder of *Panorama,* the late Dennis Bardens (1911-2004) told me of two personal experiences of a similar nature which he encountered during his long life. The first occurred in a flat in Highgate in the 1930s when he and a friend witnessed a strange electrical glow which illuminated the room and then vanished. He described this experience in his book *Ghosts and Hauntings* (1965). His second encounter with the glow took place over sixty years later, whilst in his late eighties when staying for a short break at a residential centre for writers and artists at Mount Pleasant in Surrey. Both manifestations occurred late at night in bedrooms and gave the impression of a luminous, dynamic presence involving electrical energy. In neither case could Dennis Bardens give an explanation, despite his great knowledge of psychic matters, and they remained a puzzle to him as much as Alan Brogue's experience did for him.

The Howard Hotel, 34 Great King Street

A friendly female presence known as 'Alice' is believed to haunt the ground floor of this attractive Edinburgh hotel on Great King Street. Reported phenomena, including doors opening and closing by themselves, and the sense of a presence, were recalled by a former night porter who retired in 2005. He called the invisible presence 'Alice'.

Alice may well have a taste for luxury, as she has reputedly moved through the Hanover Room, a comfortable double room located on the ground floor. Unlike many allegedly haunted places, the atmosphere in the Howard is light and cheerful and it seems that Alice is the most gentle of ghosts. Her visitations have been very mild and carry no fear for the staff or guests who have stayed in the room.

Dovecote Road, Corstorphine

Legend has long maintained that a sycamore tree in the grounds of the Dovecote along Dovecote Road in Corstorphine is haunted by a White Lady. According to legend, during the seventeenth century Christian Nimmo, the wife of a prosperous Edinburgh merchant, fell in love with James, Laird of Forrester. The couple would meet at the sycamore tree at the start of their assignations but it transpired that Christian had to compete with James's love of the bottle and the couple quarrelled. Finally, after an incident in which Christian had forced James from the comfort of a tavern, he attacked her by the sycamore tree. In turn, she pulled his sword from its scabbard and stabbed him to death.

Sentenced to death for murder, her execution was twice postponed. She was incarcerated in the Tolbooth prison and once managed to escape. But she was recaptured and beheaded on 12 November 1679. Thereafter her ghost was said return to the area around the sycamore tree, holding a sword (sadly the ancient tree itself was lost after a storm on 26 December 1998). It may be noted that the evocatively named Hunter's Tryst Inn in Edinburgh also claims a White Lady ghost; is she by any chance connected with the legend of Corstorphine?

Gillespie Hospital

Another long-told story concerns an ancient mansion named Wrychtishousis, which stood on the site of the Gillespie Hospital, later the James Gillespie School, at Bruntsfield. Following the conclusion of the American War of Independence, the building served as the town residence of Lieutenant Robertson of Lawers, a now deserted village on the banks of Loch Tay. On his return to Europe the general brought with him a black servant, known as 'Black Tom'. Tom's own room was situated on the ground floor. During his residence he was often heard to complain that he was disturbed during the night by a frightful apparition which appeared near his bed. It was a headless woman carrying a child in her arms. He said this grim spectre regularly rose up from the floor and terrified him.

Despite his protestations, little regard was given to his complaints. Although the room had an uncanny reputation, Tom was known to enjoy a drink and his vision was scorned by the rest of the household as an alcohol-induced hallucination. It is also likely that Tom suffered the fate of many ghost witnesses of the eighteenth and nineteenth centuries in having his testimony dismissed as unreliable because of his social status.

But years later there was to be a strange sequel, which many felt was a just vindication of Tom and his story. When the building was pulled down and the Gillespie Hospital constructed on the site, a box was discovered under the hearth of the room formerly occupied by Tom. On being opened it was found to contain the dressed skeleton of a woman from which the head had been severed and the bones of an infant, wrapped in a pillow case trimmed with lace. The lady was presumed to have been murdered; she had a pair of scissors hanging from a ribbon from her side and a thimble which had dropped from her finger.

This story follows a traditional pattern known since antiquity of a haunting being attributed to a person who has been denied proper funeral rights. Examples are known from classical Greece, ancient Egypt and nineteenth-century Japan as well as in British and European folklore.

Second Sight at East Ferry

On 3 May 1679, Archbishop James Sharp was travelling in a coach from Edinburgh to his home in St Andrews. He had just attended a meeting and was accompanied by his daughter and five servants in purple livery. Just as they crossed over the rough moorland track at Magus they were overtaken by a group of riders who had been planning to ambush Sheriff William Carmichael of Fife. In fact, Archbishop Sharp provided an even more prominent target: in vain the coachman tried to whip his horses but riders overtook them and cut the harness. The Archbishop was hauled from the coach and begged to be spared. One version of his death maintains that he was killed by a pistol shot fired by James Mitchell who escaped justice for a number of years, but history holds he was slain by Covenanters wielding swords who hacked him to death. A stone pyramid at Magus Muir today marks the place of the assassination.

In a rare work on second sight, Robert Barclay of Urie gave details of an incident in which he foresaw the murder of Archbishop Sharp. Some days before the murder, the devout Quaker had been travelling on horseback with his sister-in-law to a meeting of the Friends which was held annually in Edinburgh. At the East Ferry they passed a kirk which belonged to Archbishop Sharp, close by the edge of the town. As they did so they heard 'a most terrifying howling noise' in the air. They sent a servant to look through the kirk windows to see if perchance the noise was emanating from inside the building but they could see nothing

Left and above: *A haunted bedroom in the Howard Hotel visited by the most gentle of ghosts. (Photographs by Victoria Amador)*

untoward within. No sooner had the servant returned to them when the noise began again, and continued until they had travelled out of earshot. Both men gave details of their experience afterwards and repeated it to enquirers over the years. Whilst simply to repeat a story is not to corroborate it, the pair were credited with consistently telling the same story over many years.

The belief that tragic events might be foreshadowed is a long-standing one which has been the subject of controversy and interest for centuries. Sharp was detested in life by Covenanters and few would have believed that his death merited a grim supernatural warning; rather it was for the bloodshed of the battles of Drumclog and Bothwell Brig later in 1679, which proved disastrous for the Covenanters. Following his victory at Bothwell Brig the Duke of Monmouth also had five Covenanter prisoners chosen at random and taken to Magus Muir and hanged, in revenge for the Archbishop's murder.

Archbishop Sharp was buried at St Andrew's church at Fife and his marble monument depicts him kneeling to receive the crown of martyrdom, together with a Latin inscription above a relief of the Archbishop's assassination on Magus Muir. But the remains of Archbishop Sharp were fated not to rest in peace, for some thirty-six years later in 1725 rioters broke into the tomb and stole his body. It was never recovered.

A Crisis Apparition at Rutland Street

Number 36 Rutland Street was the scene of what the Society for Psychical Research considered a well-attested apparition on Christmas Eve 1887. It was experienced by an Edinburgh doctor, W.A. Jamieson, who practiced in Charlotte Square.

Dr Jamieson wrote to the Society and his letter was included in the *Census of Hallucinations*, the largest study ever undertaken of hallucinations and apparitional experience.

> I am an early riser; the awakening bell usually rings at seven o'clock a.m. On the morning of December 24th 1887, it rang a little later, about twenty minutes past seven. I was aroused by it, but did not immediately rise, though fully awake. The dawning light came in somewhat obscurely, as the shutters were partly closed. When just on the point of rising, I became conscious that a dark form, distinctly that of a female of medium height, was passing around the foot of my bed, and glided up to my side. When it reached me I raised myself in bed and felt with my hand, but it passed through the shadow. I felt nothing, and on looking closely found the apparition had gone. I at once pulled my watch from under the pillow; it was exactly half-past seven.

The doctor described his own circumstances as being just on the point of rising, being in good health, having no worry or anxiety, and being then forty-eight years old.

> The form closely resembled that of a patient of mine whom I had seen the evening before. She was very ill, though quite conscious, and I had told her husband that I did not think she would live over the night... She was aged sixty-six, was not an interesting person; had caused her friends much distress from her habits. She died as nearly as could be ascertained at 7.30 a.m. on December 24th, 1887.

Dr Jamieson awakened his wife and told her of the experience. Later that morning on calling at the house, he learned from the husband of the lady that she had died at 7.30 a.m., although subsequently her death was registered as occurring at 7.55 a.m. on the certificate; a time of eight o'clock in the morning was given by the daughter who provided a short statement to the Society in October 1891.

Further clarification arose when he was interviewed by Professor Sidgwick, who learned that Dr Jamieson was 'undoubtedly quite awake' and that he had not felt any chill or shudder when attempting to touch the figure. 'Though he knew the woman to be dying, his mind was not occupied by her.' Further confirmation of the experience came from the doctor's wife who recalled that her husband had told her of seeing the figure, although he had not then connected it with his dying patient.

The extensive literature accumulated by the Society for Psychical Research at the end of the nineteenth century showed that he was far from alone in his experience. Noting that the figure had accommodated itself to the conditions of illumination in the room at the hour it had appeared, it was considered that Dr Jamieson's apparition was 'analogous to the cloud-like stages of some hallucinations, telepathic and other, and to the shrouded forms classed with undeveloped hallucinations.' Given that Dr Jamieson was frank about his opinions on the personal deficiencies of his patient, it would certainly seem strange that he should have a hallucination of her, the only one of his entire life hitherto, close to the time she died.

The autobiographical sketch *The Life and Times of Lord Brougham* contains a similar story of Lord Chancellor Brougham's experience of the kind of phenomena which were later termed in the nineteenth and twentieth-century 'crisis apparitions'. Whilst at university, Brougham had many long discussions with a close friend whom he names only as 'G.' about the subject of ghosts, life after death and the fate of the soul. As a consequence, Brougham wrote, '…we actually committed the folly of drawing up an agreement written in our blood, to the effect that whichever of us died first should appear to the other, and thus solve any doubts we had entertained of the 'life after death'. Following college G., went to India and thereafter schoolboy intimacy faded away and the two had little contact.

In December 1799 Lord Brougham was travelling in Sweden, making for Norway. He reached an inn about 1 a.m. in the morning. Tired and cold, Lord Brougham took advantage of a hot bath to relax. As he did so he looked towards the chair on which he had placed his clothes to see G. sitting in the chair calmly looking towards him. 'How I got out of the bath, I know not, but on recovering my senses I found myself sprawling on the floor. The apparition – or whatever it was – that had taken the likeness of G., had disappeared.'

The vision made a great impression upon his lordship; he duly wrote a full account and noted the date of the appearance as 19 December, although he did not speak to anyone concerning the vision.

> I recollected quickly enough our old discussion and the bargain we had made. I could not discharge from my mind the impression that G. must have died, and that his appearance to me was to be received by me as proof of a future state; yet all the while I felt convinced that the whole was a dream; and so painfully vivid, so unfading the impression, that I could not bring myself to talk of it or make the slightest allusion to it.

Soon after Brougham's return to Edinburgh a letter arrived from India informing him of the death of G. on 19 December, the same date as his experience. The case was cited as an example of a crisis apparition by later Victorian writers on ghosts but in Scottish tradition his vision would have been hailed as an example of 'second sight'.

Above: *On the morning of Christmas Eve 1887, Dr Jamieson woke to find a shadowy figure standing at his bedside.*

Below: *Stevenson House, where the shade of the great writer Robert Louis Stevenson is said to return.*

Stevenson House, 17 Herriot Row

'I looked back into the hallway and had the distinct impression of a dark-eyed man standing there, looking at us with curiosity, not sure whether he should come forward or stay in the shadows. But it was probably my imagination.' So wrote the American ghost hunter Hans Holzer after a visit to Stevenson House in May 1973 to enquire about the ghost of Robert Louis Stevenson. The great writer lived in the house between 1857 and 1880. The then owner of the property, Mrs Kathleen MacFie maintained she felt a strong sense of the great writer's presence around the house and that he was friendly. A guest at the house, the Irish writer James Pope Hennessey said that he was sure he had seen Stevenson's ghost when he had stayed there. In fact this would have been the second encounter for the writer, for he also maintained he had seen Stevenson's apparition in Samoa on visit there. A psychic lady who accompanied Holzer stated she also sensed a presence in the house and felt herself touched by invisible fingers.

Number 17 Herriot Row was for a period a museum dedicated to the great writer but it has now reverted to a private house. Enquirers are therefore requested to respect the privacy of the occupiers and of the ghost – if he is still in residence.

SIX

HAUNTED PLACES NEAR EDINBURGH

Baberton House, Juniper Green, Balerno

Recollections by former residents of this building suggest that it was haunted throughout their occupation, though the manifestations seem to have caused little in the way of problems. 'We came to accept them as background noise', recalled one former resident. Phenomena seemed to have followed the pattern of many low-level hauntings including odd noises, footsteps and doors opening and closing by themselves. Baberton House also possessed a haunted green room – a change from the numerous 'blue rooms' found in many famous haunted houses – where a light was always burning. Often people coming back to the building at night would find it had come on, even though lights had been extinguished before they had left the property.

St Bridget's Kirk, Dalgetty Bay

The eerie ruins of the twelfth-century St Bridget's Kirk on Dalgetty Bay are reached down a rough track. Even in the daytime the place has a powerful atmosphere and it comes as no surprise to learn that the area around the ruined church and graveyard have long been said to be haunted and a meeting place for witches. On autumnal nights the ghosts of pirates, who once plagued shipping passing through the bay, are said to return. Tradition has it that the ruins were later used by body-snatching gangs, who would signal across the bay at night to Edinburgh compatriots. Their wicked practice ended after they were betrayed by one of their number. It is possible that the ghost stories of pirates were inspired by the Death's Head carvings on some of the tombs and were employed as a cover for the gang's nefarious activities, but even today only the bravest would choose to linger here after dark.

Caroline Park

Although strange noises have long been associated with Caroline Park, its most extraordinary manifestation in the nineteenth century was a haunting by what was described as a phantom cannonball! The most famous account holds that the cannonball appeared to a certain Lady John one night after she had retired to her bedroom. Suddenly she saw a black sphere burst into her room through the window. The object bumped its way across the floor with three

Above: *St Bridget's Kirk, Dalgetty Bay. (Photograph by Victoria Amador)*

Left: *An illustration of a witch from Sir Walter Scott's* Letters on Demonology and Witchcraft.

Opposite above: *St Bridget's Kirk, Dalgetty Bay. (Photograph by Victoria Amador)*

Opposite below: *Death's Head carving which may have inspired tales of pirates at St Bridget's Kirk. (Photograph by Victoria Amador)*

The Cramond Inn. (Photograph by Victoria Amador)

echoing thumps and struck the draught-screen. In great alarm, Lady John pulled upon a communication bell to summon help. Servants rushed to her aid and to comfort her, and a search was immediately conducted for the object. No trace of the cannonball could be found; there not the slightest sign of damage and the window through which the missile had been seen to fly was discovered to be intact and securely shut.

The incident might well have been dismissed as a momentary hallucination, but for the report in 1879 of a governess witnessing an identical phenomenon. She was so terrified by the experience that during the remainder of her stay at Caroline Park she would never again sit alone in the room. Nonetheless, it seems that other members of the household accepted the spectral sphere and the accompanying noise as a matter of course. Indeed, two family servants who were left in charge of the house for long periods became so accustomed to the noise that they ceased even to be alarmed at its sporadic intrusions.

Nor was all ghostly activity confined to the house. The ghost of a former Lady Royston, dressed in green robes and dripping with water, was said to rise slowly from a well in the grounds and walk across a field towards the front door of Caroline Park. She was then said to materialise in the courtyard and ring an alarm bell (long since removed). The great niece of Lady John was said to have lain awake on many occasions waiting for the ghost. Although she did not see it, she heard the ghostly tolling of the bell on nights when not a breath of wind was stirring.

The Cramond Inn, Cramond

Set on the edge of the Firth, Cramond is an ancient settlement with the remains of a Roman fort still visible. This once quiet village is fast becoming an urbanised suburb of Edinburgh with a swathe of new housing developments and an accompanying gridlock of rush-hour traffic. However, it is still possible to get a feel of the tranquillity of past times at the old Cramond Kirk and graveyard or by walking along the tree-lined edge of the Forth. Here a degree of solitude may still be enjoyed during daytime, particularly when bad weather keeps the majority at home indoors. But for those looking for the real spirit of the past inside and in comfort, the best option is the charming old Cramond Inn.

Even sceptical members of the bar staff with whom I spoke in December 2006 admitted to uncanny feelings in a certain section of the restaurant and in the top floor of the building. Whilst the pub seems warm and friendly during the day, they admitted the interior of this ancient inn can take on a very different feeling at night. There is a potent and unpleasant intensity in the darkness and one female member of staff is convinced there is a phantom woman who follows her through the pub. More routine haunted pub phenomena include the unexplained movement and breakage of glasses stacked on shelves inside the wooden bar. Another trick encountered by staff is the disappearance of salt and pepper pots which have just been laid down on

Dalkeith House has a lengthy history of manifestations. (Photograph by Victoria Amador)

tables, prior to the restaurant opening to customers. As with so many pub ghosts, those of the Cramond Inn have opted for the traditional ways of making their presence felt.

Dalkeith House

Lights going on and off by themselves, unexplained footsteps during the night and an uncomfortable atmosphere in the wine cellar and the TV room were among the ghostly experiences reported by American students from Wisconsin staying at Dalkeith House in 2006 and 2007. Students on a course based at the eighteenth-century house on the north bank of the River Esk found themselves reacting with a mixture of fear, intrigue and even amusement to the uncanny incidents. What they did not know was that strange phenomena at Dalkeith House were part of a pattern of low-level haunting stretching back many years to when it was still occupied as a stately home.

Parts of Dalkeith House are very old indeed, with its foundations dating to the twelfth century. In its history it has changed hands a number of times, being the headquarters for General Monck when Governor of Scotland under Oliver Cromwell, and afterwards owned by Anne, Duchess of Buccleuch following the execution of her husband the Duke of Monmouth, who was beheaded in 1689.

The reputation for being haunted goes back to at least the early twentieth century. In 1981, Princess Alice, Duchess of Gloucester, recorded in her memoirs that a 'spooky spot' was situated between the double doors of an upstairs dining room. Princess Alice and her sister Sybil would always link hands and run past the spot with their eyes closed. The sensation may have been more than imagination, for years later an uncle of the princess admitted experiencing a disturbing presence at the same place. Another eerie spot in the building to which dogs reacted with fear was a room in which Queen Victoria once slept. Strange noises – possibly of paranormal origin – were also heard in the house after dark.

None of this was known to students from the United States when they stayed in the building. However, their experiences suggest that whatever energies may have been active in the house when it was a family residence in the past have not dispersed.

Woodhouse Lea, Fulford

Often when seeking to trace the origins of a well-known ghost story one discovers that the tale becomes increasingly dubious the closer one gets to the original source. At worst, a popular ghost story can turn out to be wholly invented or simply pure folklore incapable of corroboration. But the reverse can also prove to be the case. The story of the Woodhouse Lea ghost provides a good example of how garbled folklore may turn out to have a basis in a real experience.

Confusion has arisen about the original location of the haunting at Woodhouse Lea. Sources are confused as to whether it occurred around the fragmentary remains of the old castle or at the later Woodhouse Lea House at Fulford, itself since demolished.

One version has the ghost of a White Lady (or alternatively a Green Lady) wandering the woods around the ruins of one or other of the sites. When the castle was largely demolished, it has been said that the ghost was transferred along with the stones and timbers used to build the new house. In some accounts – and most unusually for a ghost – she is naked. During the Second World War, Woodhouse Lea was used as a prisoner of war camp and there were reports of sentries seeing and challenging the ghost on some fourteen occasions. Stories also circulated that when the snow lay thick upon the ground strange footprints appeared. Another claim was that the ghost of Lady Hamilton was said to be heard knocking on the north-east door in the depths of winter, but as with most folktales, no first-hand witnesses could be located.

Nonetheless, it seems claims of a haunting at the later Woodhouse Lea House were based upon genuine manifestations. A letter dating from 1886 and preserved by the Society for Psychical Research reveals that there were at least two witnesses to strange noises in the house. In the spring of 1875 two sisters, Bessie and Laurie Craigie, occupied a bedroom together in a new wing which had been added to the house. The room was situated at the end of a passage some distance from the other bedrooms and the two sisters were the first people to occupy the room.

According to Bessie the pair were awoken simultaneously during the night by a knock at the door. At first they thought it was a housemaid come to call them. Then they realised that the room was completely dark. Laurie called to her sister, 'It can't be the housemaid coming to call, who can it be?' No one attempted to enter. Then, as Bessie described it, 'we heard a deep sigh, footsteps going swiftly along the passage away from our door, rather to our relief.'

The Craigie sisters lay awake but heard no further sounds. Later Bessie was even able to make a bit of a joke about the incident with her sister, saying, 'It was mean of you to call out "come in" to a ghost for I was next to the door!'

The sisters relayed their experience the next morning at breakfast. The family seemed rather pleased and interpreted the incident as the ghost 'showing approval'. Although the Craigie sisters did not encounter the ghost again, they learned that their host family had many stories about the haunting. Family members had rarely seen it, but they had often heard the sound of someone walking along the passageway, knocking at doors and then hastening away. Later, in an unidentified book devoted to 'Haunted Houses', Bessie Craigie found an account claiming that the old Woodhouse Lea site was said to be haunted by a phantom of a woman whose child was frozen to death in the snow after mother and infant were turned out of her house naked by raiders on a winter's night.

One version of this story details the events as having taken place in the winter of 1569 and identifies the women as Lady Anne Hamilton, wife of James Hamilton of Bothwellhaugh. He was absent from the house that night but was the real target of the attack. The identity of the raider is given as Regent Moray, James Stewart, half-brother of Mary Queen of Scots, or one of his henchmen. In revenge James Hamilton instigated the killing of Regent Moray at Linlithgow on 23 January 1570. Hamilton was then in turn executed, whilst his wife lived on, insane, until her own death in 1609.

Some eighty years after the Craigie sisters wrote their account for the Society for Psychical Research there were reports of a White Lady being glimpsed in the building, not long before its demolition. In January 1964 a Mr Ian Groat and two friends saw a fluorescent form moving back and forth in the by-now derelict property for nearly five minutes. After demolition, the apparition of a woman in white was also reported by stable girls working in a stable block on the edge of the estate. Tradition still holds that the ghost may be encountered walking in the woods, particularly over the turn of the year.

Restalrig Loch, Lochend

Lying to the east of Edinburgh, Restalrig Loch is mentioned in Sir Walter Scott's *Letters on Demonology and Witchcraft*. Scott tells how a sixteenth-century lady named Elizabeth or Bessie Dunlop declared that as she went to tether her horse at the loch she heard a tremendous sound like a body of riders rushing past her. The invisible presences seemed to gallop straight into the waters of the loch accompanied by a hideous rumbling sound. Bessie maintained that the noises were attributable to spirits (or perhaps fairy beings) passing by in a great number, bringing to mind the ancient belief of classical philosophers such as Poseidonius who held that the spirits of the dead dwelt in the air in vast numbers. A further remarkable feature of her account was the source of her information on the cause of the sound: she maintained it came from a personal spirit guide, her sincere belief in the reality of whom was to cost Bessie her life.

Bessie openly claimed she was in touch with the spirit of a soldier named Thome Reid who had supposedly died at the Battle of Pinkie on 10 September 1547. Bessie went on to describe Thome Reid in detail, saying that he appeared to her as an elderly, grey-bearded man in a Lombard coat, grey breeches, white stockings gartered above the knee and a black bonnet on his head. In one hand he held a white wand.

The spirit of Reid duly directed her on various matters and could tell her, in the case of sick persons, who would die and who would recover. She averred that Thome Reid gave her advice on medical cures for other sick people who consulted her. There was no evidence that the advice of the alleged Thome Reid resulted in harm to anyone (Scott observes that he appeared to maintain a theological line in keeping with orthodox Catholic views of the time). No one in her defence was prepared to cite from St Paul's second letter to the Corinthians, which states that the ability to distinguish between good and bad spirits is a gift of the Holy Spirit, or to argue (as Sir Walter Scott considered) that she was suffering from a disease of the mind. Although there was no evidence that her actions had harmed anyone, she was found guilty of sorcery. Bessie Dunlop was burned as a witch on 8 November 1576.

Reading the confessions of Bessie Dunlop today provides a fascinating example of a person who might be better described as a spirit medium rather than a witch. Although Scott's

Above: *Hopetoun House. (Photograph by Victoria Amador)*

Opposite: *The Leith Hall haunting was extensively covered in the press in the 1960s.*

explanation might still be applied to someone claiming such otherworldly encounters, it must be said her account prefigures by some three centuries the accounts of nineteenth-century spiritualists who claimed to have personal spirit guides as well as those of 'channellers' today who assert the same.

Hopetoun House

What has been described as Scotland's grandest stately home, standing on the south shore of the Forth, was built at the turn of the nineteenth century by the first Earl of Hopetoun, whose family were later created the Marquesses of Linlithgow. Enlarged in 1721 by William Adam, the house was given its magnificent frontage, colonnades and state apartments; as well as lavish decoration and ceiling paintings, the house contains extensive collections of porcelain and pictures, including works by Gainsborough and fine furniture. In 1974 a charitable trust was created to preserve both the house and its contents in perpetuity. However, it is not within the fine interior of the mansion that the family ghost manifests but outside amongst its spacious grounds.

The house is set in 100 acres of rolling parkland, including woods and numerous picnic spots. The apparition is a man clad in back who appears on a certain path in the garden, shunned by those who know of its significance, for the ghost is considered to be a harbinger of death and disaster for the family.

The story was well known into the twentieth century. In 1981, the then Marchioness of Linlithgow recalled that there was always a certain spot which she avoided with her brothers and sister on account of its unpleasant atmosphere. On one occasion she recalled that she was walking in the grounds when her dogs began to react at an unseen presence, 'and were obviously following something that they could see and we could not'. One of the animals even appeared to be trying to snap at something, as if trying to bite at invisible legs or ankles. She revealed that a disaster for the family had followed within twenty-four hours of the strange incident and that thereafter she always tried to avoid the same spot and to hurry past if in the vicinity.

Leith Hall

Although a considerable distance from the city, Leith Hall was on the itinerary of every American ghost hunter to Edinburgh in the 1960s and early 1970s. The sound of funeral drums and many voices singing Mass were among the experiences of Elizabeth Byrd, an American novelist and writer who lived with her husband Barrie Gaunt at Leith Hall in the 1960s. Elizabeth Byrd was the authoress of the book *A Strange and Seeing Time* which detailed a number of her psychic experiences and impressions. Both she and her husband were convinced there were haunting presences in their home and were prepared to entertain ghost hunters and psychic investigators. Elizabeth Byrd was later to have further experiences at her next home at Monckton Tower in the 1970s (see below).

Once, when Barrie Gaunt was showing visitors around the hall, he opened a door in a small room to see what he described as, 'a dear old lady fussing around a table. She was dressed in Victorian fashion. The tourists couldn't see her, but I could. However, I left her at peace'. Perhaps it was the old lady who was responsible for the mysterious appearance of objects which baffled the couple on occasion. Barrie Gaunt discovered an old leather writing case in his desk draw. 'I was flabbergasted. I was using that draw day in and day out and the writing case, had it been there all along, was so big I just couldn't have missed it.' Elizabeth Byrd was equally puzzled by the mysterious appearance of two tea cosies in her study. 'The door had been locked and neither Barrie nor Phyllis, the maid, was responsible' she told a journalist.

Amongst the outsiders who experienced phenomena was Iain Parr, a journalist for the *Weekly Scotsman* who visited the house in April 1967. He encountered 'something' that pulled him from his pillow in a guest room. 'I was lying in bed, eyes wide open and my hands behind my head, staring up at the ceiling. The witching hour had chimed from the clock on the staircase and the moon came out with her pale, sad light from behind the clouds.' However, his thoughts as he recalled them were actually on the Spanish conquest of the Incas, '…when suddenly I was PULLED up into a sitting position. It was quite involuntary on my part. Whatever it was I was allowed to flop back.' He at once switched on the light and found his pyjama jacket apparently untouched and nothing to be seen.

The following year, on 16 July 1968, Elizabeth Byrd saw a bearded man in green breeches in the house at a time her husband was away. In an account she gave to the American ghost hunter Hans Holzer, she described the man having a bandage across the head and holding a short, blunt weapon. Elizabeth screamed, 'Go away!' and the figure, seemingly in response, backed away and disappeared into a mirror. Considerably shaken she fled the room but the figure did not appear again.

Monckton Tower, Old Craig Hall

The ancient Monckton Tower at Old Craig Hall, Musselburgh was haunted by a ghostly monk and a woman in white, according to Elizabeth Byrd who rented the property in the early 1970s. The site had been the home of an order of monks in the past and if experiences reported by Elizabeth Byrd and by visitors – many of whom claimed psychic abilities themselves – are accepted, it seems that the monks must have eaten well.

Phantom smells were experienced by Elizabeth Byrd and her guests on various occasions. She described (perhaps with an excess of zeal worthy of a cookery programme) 'a marvellous juicy kind of baking of meat, or the roasting of meat which seemed to emanate from the old stone fireplace… It wasn't the kind of meat you get in the supermarket: it was more like standing rib roast – expensive gorgeous meat.'

Another psychic lady named Alanna Knight also claimed to have experienced delicious smells of cooking and, on one occasion early in the morning, she also heard the tolling of a church bell. In fact, there was no church bell within miles of the site. More difficult to explain, in light of the building's monastic history, was the experience of another guest, a Mr Boyd, who saw a woman in a long and dirty-looking white dress appear in the bedroom one night in April 1972. It seems most probable that she was she was a shade from a later era. Later the same year, in the early hours of the morning of 27 December 1972, a medium named Ian Adam encountered a distinct smell of rosemary and sensed a lady engaged in cooking – perhaps a cook or housekeeper for the brethren who once occupied the site?

Lauriston House

Set just within the boundaries of the city, Lauriston House is haunted by phantom footsteps. Although called a castle, the building is in fact a sixteenth-century house with neo-Jacobean turrets and gables, with further domestic extensions added in the nineteenth century. It was given to the city of Edinburgh in 1926 by its last private owners, Mr and Mrs Reid. The Reids had filled the building with a wide range of treasures and art objects. The terms of the gift were that everything should be preserved without any change or alteration. These instructions have been followed and a visit to Lauriston Castle, which commands fine views over the Firth of Forth, is like stepping inside a time capsule. It may also be hoped that the strict preservation policy has also retained the ghost which was active soon after the ownership of the house was passed on. One of the most detailed accounts of the phantom footsteps came five years after it was acquired by the city: it was from a Mr John Fairley who stayed alone in the castle one night in 1931.

Nothing disturbed John Fairley's slumbers until after midnight, when he was awakened by the sound of someone approaching his room from along the passage. He could distinctly make out the curious shuffling sound of feet moving in loose slippers. On reaching the right-angle turning in the corridor, he noticed there was a pause. He sat up in bed and at that moment thought the apparition was about to enter the room. Switching on a small electric torch which he always placed under his pillow, he swept the beam of the torch around the room but saw nothing. Hearing nothing further, he relaxed and before long was again fast asleep.

Up until this point, the account resembles the behaviour of ghosts at other locations mentioned in this book, notably Woodhouse Lea and Grange House. However, Mr Fairley's sleep was to be disturbed again by what was described as 'the most appalling crash he had ever heard in his life as if a bomb had struck the roof and exploded close to his bedside.' He lay perfectly still for a few minutes, thinking about what to do next, but all was quiet. Switching on his torch, he shone its beam around the room. A large heavy picture had fallen from the wall above the washstand and struck glass utensils below. Remarkably cool, Fairley nonetheless turned over and went back to sleep.

Telling his story to another curator the next day, he stated his belief that the fall of the picture had nothing to do with the unexplained footsteps. Would the falling picture really have resulted in the 'most appalling crash he had ever heard in his life'? Perhaps, for sounds do often seem louder during the still of the night. Yet in a number of cases recorded by psychic researchers, loud inexplicable bangs and crashes have been accompanied by the unexplained movement of objects. As to the footsteps at Lauriston House, tradition attributes them to the ghost of an old family butler wearing slippers, though his precise identity is a mystery.

Lauriston House is haunted by the sound of the footsteps of a butler wearing slippers. (Photograph by Victoria Amador)

Liberton Hall

A strange photograph taken in the 1890s at Liberton Hall fascinated the 3rd Marquess of Bute, John Patrick Crichton Stuart (1847-1900). The Marquess was a wealthy landowner, a talented historian and archaeologist and a benefactor of Glasgow and St Andrews University. He was also actively interested in psychic issues and became vice president of the Society for Psychical Research. Among the many strange stories which he investigated across Scotland was a mysterious photograph taken at Liberton Hall which he considered showed the face of an apparition.

The L-shaped building was originally built by William Little, Provost of Edinburgh in the early seventeenth century. By the end of the nineteenth century it was being rented out and the tenant during the 1890s employed a professional photographer to take a picture of some of the interesting features in one of the chambers. These included an ancient nail-studded door frame with a recess above. When the photograph was developed there appeared in the top left-hand corner above the recess an image like a face.

Opposite: *Isolated Penkaet House had a playful invisible ghost in the twentieth century. (Photograph by Victoria Amador)*

Left: *The Marquess of Bute (1847-1900) who investigated the ghost of Liberton Hall.*

Lord Bute showed the photograph to Abbot Sir David Hunter Blair O.S.B. who many years later published details in the Catholic paper, *The Universe*. The picture was considered to show what was described as, 'the presentment of a huge human face – not uncomely, with a well-shaped nose, down-turned eyes under strongly marked eyebrows, and a mouth (whether or not shaded by a moustache is uncertain), wearing a smile as inscrutable and enigmatical as the Mona Lisa.'

Sir David asked Lord Bute, 'Do you suppose that he is dead?' to which his lordship replied, 'No, he is not dead; but he is saying "I know more than you do". This rather cryptic remark might reflect a belief in a ghost of the living on the part of Lord Bute (he was once said to have appeared as a ghost himself) or reflect the view of survival after death.

Sir David was sufficiently interested in the image to visit Liberton House with Sir Robert Gordon-Gilmour and examine the scene of the haunting but could see nothing 'except a stretch of dirty and discoloured plaster'. The photograph was also submitted to other photographers for analysis. Whilst not prepared to state that the image was that of a ghost, they expressed the opinion that it was unlikely that the plate had been used before (i.e. it was not a double exposure) and stated, 'We are glad to have had the opportunity of seeing what is, beyond doubt, a distinct curiosity.' The story was published in the 1950s in Sir Shane Leslie's *Ghost Book*, a work which examines ghostly experiences from a Catholic perspective.

Curiously, not everyone was able to make out the face as clearly as Lord Bute or Sir David, showing there is a strong subjective element to the interpretation of anomalous images. Although there are pictures from spiritualist circles from the 1860s onwards (the medium the Revd Stainton Moses had personally examined some 600 alleged spirit photographs as early as 1875), the Liberton House picture was one of the first examples of a spontaneous image obtained in an ancient property. Belief – or hope – that psychic impressions can be recorded in photographs persists to this day.

Interestingly, Lord Bute's own death was said to have been heralded by a ghostly warning. On the eve of her father's death, 8 October 1900, Lady Margaret MaCrae, his only daughter, heard the

sound of an invisible carriage outside Dumfries House which was recognised as a death portent in the family. Since the early 1990s there have also been sporadic accounts of strange phenomena at Liberton Hall including lights switching themselves on and off and dogs barking at something unseen.

Penkaet House, Pentcaitland

During the 1940s and 1950s the rather remote Penkaet House (also known as Penkaet Castle and Fountain Hall) at Pentcaitland became internationally known for its invisible but highly active ghost. It was occupied by a family named Holbourn, whose members were happy to talk about their experiences.

Traditionally, the house possessed a rich and motley collection of phantoms spanning the social order. They ranged from a ghostly King Charles I to a beggar named Hamilton, supposedly executed as a wizard. Much as any owner or visitor would have delighted in these colourful spooks, it was the better-attested accounts of an unseen presence capable of poltergeist tricks which attracted the attention of ghost hunters, including researchers from the American Society for Psychical Research.

The Holbourn family attributed the unusual incidents to the ghost of John Cockburn, a past owner who was said to have murdered John Seton, to whom his family were related. It seems the Holbourns may have preferred this story of John to the tale of a beggar and wizard named Hamilton who was reputed to have cursed the building and been executed on Castle Hill in Edinburgh for sorcery. The story of a wizard who bewitches premises which become afflicted by poltergeist effects is not unknown (another example is the seventeenth-century 'Demon Drummer of Tedworth' in Wiltshire). It may be that the legend grew up to explain the ghost, or it could be the threat of his powers triggered subconscious reactions in the occupants.

Whichever was the case, it seems the Holbourns were prepared to treat their invisible presence as a personality in its own right and accept the incidents as a matter of course.

On occasion the ghost could be responsive. Alasdair Alpin MacGregor recorded that, 'he has confined himself to creating in various parts of the house knocking noises, to which the inmates are now so accustomed that they pay no attention to them, except, perhaps when they become too persistent… when John indulges in a bout of knocking, he is apt to continue until some member of the Holbourn family requests him to desist, which he does immediately.'

In 1946 the American Society for Psychical Research covered the haunting at Penkaet House in their *Journal*. In the spring of that year, a party from the Edinburgh College of Art stayed at the castle over a weekend whilst rehearsing a play. In statements collected by the American SPR, witnesses identified simply as Miss Jocelyn L.S. and Miss Pat M.T. stated that about midnight they heard an extraordinary noise, 'like something trundling across the floor' of the room above the King Charles Room or library. They further described it as being 'like something going down a slope'. The noise came repeatedly and they also heard footsteps in the room above. These were attributed to a Mr Brown; he told them that he had been fast asleep at the time.

One of the visitors had with her a square travelling clock which failed to work during its time in the building. This prompted Mr Houlbourn to observe that no clock would go if placed on the wall between the dining room and the next room. The strange effect was also experienced with watches hung upon the same wall.

Strange incidents went back some years. At midnight on Christmas Eve 1923 the family were sitting around the fire and singing carols together, celebrating their first Christmas at Penkaet. Leaning on the fireplace stood a plaque with the family crest which suddenly lent forward, as though bowing to company! It remained in this position for several seconds before reverting to its normal position.

One night in 1935 Alasdair Holbourn was quietly reading by the sitting room fire when the maid entered to ask whether he was having a bath. Somebody appeared to be running bath water. Alasdair assured the maid that he was not responsible and suggested that perhaps the children's nurse was responsible. However, the nurse had been in bed for over an hour. When Alasdair checked the bathroom he found it to be empty but full of steam. A strange piece of soap 'the like of which he had never seen before' was lying in the bath. Although declaring herself a sceptic, Mrs Holbourn said that she sometimes heard noises from the King's Room at night. On a more personal note, she recalled that on the night of her husband's funeral she had distinctly heard footsteps coming down the path to the house.

The American SPR also noted an account that on 29 July 1946 a glass case in the library reportedly disintegrated without apparent cause in the presence of nearly 100 members of an East Lothian society visiting the castle. In another and more detailed account of this incident it appears that the society in question was the well-respected East Lothian Antiquarian and Field Naturalist Society on a summer outing. The glass case which suddenly split open contained a model of Penkaet Castle.

However, a mundane explanation for this incident was revealed in a feature article by Alasdair Alpin MacGregor for *Country Life* magazine in December 1954; in considering the incident one could 'append the subsequent confession of a cleaner who owned to having cracked the shade, and stuck it up so it might not be noticed'.

Reporters drawn to the house were accommodated in the haunted bed and wrote rather mocking articles afterwards, but this did not undermine the acceptance of something strange in the house by members of the household.

The fantastic interior of Rosslyn Chapel.

On occasion the ghost could be a helpful presence, as when Mrs Holbourn found that a pair of pet lambs had made their way into a bedroom and settled on a four-poster. She quickly started to shoo them away out of the room and down the stairs, whereupon the massive, heavy studded door slammed behind them, preventing the animals from coming in again. Mrs Holbourn recalled that she had never known the door to previously slam of its own accord; meanwhile the lambs were gambolling away up the drive.

Since the 1950s nothing further has been heard of the invisible ghost of Penkaet Hall. Today it is an isolated private house with a sense of tranquillity, so it may be that the ghost has departed for good.

Rosslyn Chapel

Rosslyn Chapel, seven miles from Edinburgh, features in numerous mysteries and traditions, both ancient and modern. Some are genuine, whilst others are synthetic but clearly represent things which many deeply wish to be true, including the conspiracy theories contained in Dan Brown's novel *The Da Vinci Code*. The surge in interest in Rosslyn triggered by the novel has meant substantial investment in visitor facilities at the chapel, quite beyond what the small group of dedicated trustees who maintain the structure could ever have imagined.

The chapel was built at the instigation of Sir William St Clair, the third and last Prince of Orkney, between 1450 and 1490. During construction Sir William employed the services of skilled masons from all over Europe. The elaborate nature of their workmanship and carving has

A ghostly glow at Rosslyn Chapel was believed to herald a death in the St Clair family.

long been cited as evidence that the chapel is more than just a simple family chapel. Without doubt, the chapel is one of the most curious churches anywhere in Britain but its strange decoration is probably due to the combined efforts of masons working in accordance with their own national styles, rather than it being an enormous three-dimensional code which, if deciphered, will lead to some ultimate secret or revelation.

Nonetheless, many mystery seekers hope that the lost Gospels appropriated from the Temple of Solomon lay buried within. Some maintain that the chapel contains secrets in its stone work which will lead to spiritual revelation. It has even been suggested that the names 'Ros' and 'Lyn' have their roots in Gaelic words meaning ancient knowledge and down the ages. Another fascinating – if unlikely – idea is that carved cubes represent a secret musical notation awaiting decipherment. Others link the chapel with the Knights Templar or have even suggested that it serves as the resting place for the Holy Grail. It seems the fantastic carved imagery of the chapel leads many creative and imaginative people to project their fantasies upon it.

Not surprisingly there are ghost stories too. Festooned with wreaths of stone work is a column known as the 'Prentice Pillar' and, according to legend, the man who carved it was murdered. The story avers that a master mason apparently doubted his skill was sufficient to complete the pillar to the standard. As a result he took a pilgrimage to Rome, his intention being to seek initiation into the mysteries of art and sculpture to the greatest degree possible. During his absence in Rome his skilled apprentice took it upon himself to complete the pillar, and did so in such a skilful and exemplary fashion that people flocked to see it. His master, on returning, grew very jealous and angry that his reputation had been eclipsed by his pupil.

In a fit of rage he murdered his pupil, who cursed him as he lay dying. Thereafter, what was considered a permanent bloodstain remained at the spot, which was haunted by the apparition of the young man. In fulsome language, Elliot O'Donnell claimed in 1939 that, 'Its white, bloodstained face used to appear from behind the pillar and peer, with large troubled eyes, at people visiting the chapel, to their, doubtless, unmitigated terror.'

A strange ghostly light was also said to appear above the chapel prior to the death of a member of the St Clair family. To qualify for the spectral appearance, the dying person had to be a direct descendent of the chapel founder William St Clair, Prince of Orkney and Duke of Oldenburgh.

Sir Walter Scott recorded the tradition in his poem, *The Lay of the Last Minstrel*:

O'er Roslin all that dreary night
A wondrous blaze was seen to gleam;
Twas broader than the watch-fire light
And redder than the bright moonbeam

It glared on Roslin's castled rock,
It ruddied all the copse-wood glen
'Twas seen from Dryden's groves of oak,
And seen from caverned Hawthornden

Seemed all on fire that chapel proud
Where Roslin's chief's uncoffin'd lie;
Each baron, for a sable shroud,
Sheathed in his iron panoply.

Seemed all on fire, within, around,
Deep sacristy and altars pall;
Shone every pillar, foliage
And glimmered all the dead men's mail

Blazed battlement and pennet high
Blazed evry rose-carved buttress fair –
So still they blaze when fate is nigh
The lordly line of high St Clair

Recently, actors preparing for *A Midsummer Night's Dream* had their rehearsal 'livened up' by ghostly happenings. One actor claimed to have seen – appropriately enough – what he described as 'a fairy like figure' near the chapel. Sounds of voices have also been heard in the building before and since. In July 2005 Simon Beattie, a tour guide at the chapel, told reporters, 'Last year we were rehearsing for a fringe show and when I was locking up I heard a child's voice in the crypt and so I shouted down that I was locking up. When I went down there, however, there was no one there.'

Yet another story from the area tells how a certain aristocratic lady was jilted at the altar at Rosslyn Chapel. Her ghost is now said to haunt Blaires Hall on Polton Road, Lonehead, gazing wistfully out in the direction of the chapel. The last sighting of her is said to have been just after the Second World War when she was seen by the mother of my informant who lived at Blaires Hall as a child.

Details of the carvings in Rosslyn. (Photographs by Victoria Amador)

The entrance to Saltoun Hall today.

Saltoun Hall

With parts of historic Saltoun Hall near Pentcaitland dating back to 1220, it is not surprising that it should claim a ghost or two. Oliver Cromwell is said to have hanged ten men from its battlements during the Battle of Dunbar and many books on Scottish hauntings declare it to be haunted by a Grey Lady. Regrettably, most books are vague as to her identity, and precious few authors appear to be aware of the numerous manifestations at the hall during the mid-twentieth century.

From 1643 until 1966 the hall was occupied by the Fletcher family. When the Fletchers departed it stood empty for many months, despite being offered at a rent of £6 a week for the hall and its 44-acre estate; no tenants could be found. One factor was the repairs and redecoration, estimated at the time as requiring between £3,000-4,000. The cost of heating was also considerable – one local tale claimed that it took half a ton of coal a day to heat it. This would have been no trouble to the Fletcher family, who had once owned local coal mines. But, according to locals, tenants were more put off by the Fletcher family ghost than the cost of upkeep.

In March 1967, Patricia Troon, a reporter for the *Weekly Scotsman*, stated that, 'Even by daylight the Hall is sinister. Its windows are blinded by shutters, its enormous empty rooms echo the scuttling of mice and the creaking of time'. Her impressions were strengthened by stories given to her by Mrs Helen Addison, who had been housekeeper at the hall for thirteen years. Whilst Mrs Addison had not seen the ghost, she was convinced the building was haunted.

Possible candidates as to the identity of the ghost include Katherine Bruce who, after the death of her husband, Robert Fletcher, never left her room. She remained in a state of perpetual mourning, wearing only black until her death some thirty years afterwards. The traditional contender, however, remains Lady Milton, another Fletcher, who is said to be looking for pearls which she lost in her lifetime (she was noted to be the only female of the Fletcher line depicted in a portrait while not wearing pearls).

It appears to have been the shade of Lady Milton who frightened a parlour maid during the 1950s or early 1960s. From the details the distressed woman was able to provide, the apparition resembled a portrait of Lady Milton hanging in the dining room. Another witness was the butler, who saw the figure in Lady Milton's room.

Another phenomenon suggestive of the presence linked with Lady Milton was the fact that an old servant's bell in her chamber was known on occasion to ring by itself, although disconnected. 'Yet everyone who lived at the Hall has heard at sometime this bell ringing'.

Mrs Addison and her family also had first-hand experience of the manifestations when they occupied part of the hall which had been Lady Milton's apartments. Like so many other hauntings, there was the feeling of an invisible guest in the building. Footsteps were frequently heard by members of the family. Mrs Addison recalled that her daughter often used to wake up in the night and say someone was standing beside the bed. Her husband also reported a strange sensation: whenever he looked in a mirror, he said someone was looking over his shoulder. Mrs Addison further stated, 'One night, after I had gone upstairs to bed my family heard footsteps on the stairs and my husband came out to see why I had come downstairs again. He found that by then I was safely tucked up in bed but the footsteps were still echoing along the corridor.'

The Addisons did not consider the presence disturbing, 'Oddly enough we were never afraid. It was a Fletcher ghost and we were looking after Fletcher family and property. It meant no harm to anyone.' Today, Saltoun Hall may be glimpsed through the trees, the entrance to it being marked as 'strictly private'.

Railway Tunnel, Auchidinny

Some eight miles from Edinburgh in the Firth Woods at Auchidinny lies an abandoned railway tunnel. Both the tunnel and the area around are reputed to be haunted by a woman who was jilted by her lover and who drowned herself in the nearby River Esk. Her ghost is said to haunt the tunnel, running through to Dalmor Mill. American ghost hunter Hans Holzer, who researched the case in 1973, recorded the sighting by an Edinburgh woman who had been walking through the tunnel and encountered a female figure whose 'clothes showed her to be from an earlier period.' The figure suddenly vanished and the lady – who had previously been a sceptic – returned to Edinburgh 'in a very shaken condition'. Since then other people walking through the railway tunnel have felt a strong sense of fear at its centre.

Linlithgow Palace

It is not surprising that the gaunt remains of the once splendid palace of Linlithgow, birthplace of Mary Queen of Scots, are said to be haunted. The body of the murdered Regent Moray (see Woodhouse Lea) was taken into the palace following his assassination in January 1570. James VI also used the palace as a halting place and when driven from Edinburgh by outbreaks of plague. The last king to sleep in the palace was Charles I in 1633. The last Scottish National Parliament before the twenty-first century was held here in 1646 and thereafter it was occupied by the forces of Oliver Cromwell between 1651 to 1659. Prince Charles Edward stayed here in 1745 and George V held court here in 1914. It is now in the care of the National Trust for Scotland.

A legend claims that the ghost of an old man in a long blue gown appeared in a vision to King James IV at St Michael's church in Linlithgow and told him that he would die at the battle of Flodden: he failed to heed the warning and died in battle in 1513. His widowed Queen is said to haunt Linlithgow Palace. Another tradition holds that it is also haunted by Mary Guise, wife of James V, who appears in Queen Margaret's Bower. Yet others suggest that it is a 'Queen Margaret'. A phantom lady in a blue gown is also said to appear walking towards the church, with 9 a.m. in the morning in the months of April and September being the most favoured times for her apparition.

Alan Steel Asset Management, Linlithgow

In the autumn of 2006 a priest was called in by a company chairman following unusual phenomena at the offices of an asset-management firm in Linlithgow, Lothian. Several of the forty staff at offices of Alan Steel Asset Management have reported the unexplained figure of an elderly man walking about, strange voices and minor poltergeist phenomena. Leslie Dick, Mr Steel's PA, stated, 'I was typing the code into the key pad to open the main door and heard a man saying, "Excuse me," but there was no one there.' Another staff member Elaine Henderson was quoted as saying, 'I can definitely feel a presence when sitting in reception – not a nasty one but something is there.' Books are also reported to have fallen without explanation from shelves and been thrown around. Staff attributed the manifestations to the ghost of a foreman killed in an explosion at a factory on the site in the early twentieth century.

The Phantom Lorry Of Stow

One sunny morning in 1956, Mrs May Caig of Watherston farm at Stow was chopping wood when she became aware of a moving object in her peripheral vision. Looking around, she was astonished to see a lorry travelling along a rough sheep track unsuitable for vehicles and coming towards her. As she did so she noticed what she described as 'an evil-looking man' at the wheel. 'She was so startled that she dropped her axe and jumped aside to watch the vehicle travel down towards the Edinburgh-Stow road. It crossed Watherston Hill and Gala Water to join the main road.'

Almost as astonished were her husband and neighbours, who saw May Caig suddenly drop her axe and leap aside as though avoiding something, but they could neither see or sense anything untoward. She later gave an account of her experience to Alasdair Alpin MacGregor which he published in his book *Phantom Footsteps* the following year. May Caig might have been minded to dismiss the apparition as a bizarre hallucination but for the fact that a few weeks later stories circulated of a phantom lorry being seen on the A7 road to Edinburgh which were published in the press.

According to John Harries, who undertook a major study of haunted roads and highways across the UK in the mid-1960s, the vehicle appeared after Stow and as far as the junction for Heriot, in the valley of Gala Water. As well as manifesting on the road it would also appear on 'adjacent tracks and running across streams unsuitable for anything but a tank.' The phantom lorry was much feared and blamed for causing accidents in the area; motorists followed the lorry into a wall at a bend in the road.

Although rare, apparitions of cars and vehicles are not unknown in the literature of psychical research but perhaps as few as one in every 300 visual ghosts involve phantom vehicles. The spectral lorry was interesting in another respect, in that a phantom driver was seen at the wheel. In most other accounts vehicles seem to lack either drivers or passengers, adding to the mystery of what they are or may represent.

Shiel Hill House Hotel

Set out in the countryside, the Shiel Hill Hotel provides a delightfully pleasant and tranquil retreat of an afternoon. Certainly, the hotel does not have the feel of a haunted place and in the winter months is a warm and delightful place to take afternoon tea or other refreshment by an open fire. However, stories have long averred that the hotel has a haunted bedroom visited by a White Lady, particularly when snow is falling. The hotel staff will reveal it to interested guests who fancy an apparitional encounter.

The traditions of White Lady ghosts are widespread, being found throughout the British Isles. In recent years the hypothesis has been advanced that spectral White Ladies apparitions may be a form of archetypal hallucination, representing the *genus loci* or 'spirit of a place'. Rather than arising from the personality of a particular deceased individual, such apparitions seem to be closer to an idea or symbol. Apparitions such as White Ladies seem to be associated with particular places which trigger responses at a deep level of consciousness in the form of visions or waking dreams.

Conceivably such apparitions may be a construction of the unconscious mind stimulated by psychic forces operating both internally and externally to the brain of the witness. Such apparitions are subjective in that they exist within the mind of the observer but they also appear to have a degree of objective existence in that they recur at the same place to a succession of different witnesses, sometimes many years apart. The psychologist Carl Gustav Jung considered that, 'It not infrequently happens that the archetype appears in the form of a spirit in dreams or fantasy-products, or even

Left: *Linlithgow Palace. (Photograph by Victoria Amador)*

Below: *A White Lady haunts Shiel Hill Hotel when the snow is falling.*

comports itself like a ghost.' Could the White Lady of Shiel Hill be such an apparition? Was she even perhaps an omen for the family who lived at the house long ago?

Melville Castle

A mile and half west from Dalkeith and left largely derelict until major refurbishment in the 1990s, Melville Castle is now a delightful thirty-room hotel. The hotel stands in a 50-acre park and the restoration gives an idea of what it must have been like in its prime, having been visited variously by the great lover of luxury King George IV, Sir Walter Scott and later Queen Victoria. It is also not shy about its reputation for being haunted. The castle was built by the Rennie family in 1705 and passed by Viscount Melville, Henry Dundas. The ghost is believed to be Elizabeth, the wife of his successor William Dundas.

During restoration, owner William Hay saw a female apparition passing through the building and disappearing into a wall.

The banks of the Esk at Lasswade are haunted by a ghostly light.

Later, during the course of the renovation, a bricked-up doorway was discovered, the obvious presumption being that this was the route which the ghost walked in life. Guests seem on the whole disappointed not have encountered the female phantom. However, it may be a case of restoration and building work having disturbed old place memories, locked in the fabric of the building, generating the experience of apparitions for a short period.

Lasswade, Banks of the River Esk

Lasswade, near Dalkeith, has many literary associations. A large cottage here was the home of Sir Walter Scott for the first six years of his life. A greater lover of supernatural tales and romance, it is interesting to speculate what Sir Walter would have made of the reputed glowing ghost who haunts the district.

It is not unknown for apparitions to appear in the open air and the banks of the River Esk are said to be haunted by one of the most notorious literary drug addicts of the nineteenth century, Thomas De Quincey. De Quincey was the author of *Confessions of an Opium Eater*, detailing his hallucinations and life as a drug addict; he had a cottage here, where he spent the last nineteen years of his life. His ghost is said to wander the banks of the river in the early morning carrying a lantern. One wonders how reliable the identification may have been or whether it is an attribution of personality to an otherwise strange glowing light which might have many other possible causes or meanings. Whatever the case, the presence has chosen a delightful spot to haunt.

SELECT BIBLIOGRAPHY

Adams, Norman, *Haunted Scotland* (1998) Mainstream Publishing.
Bone, James, *The Perambulator in Edinburgh* (1926) Jonathan Cape Ltd.
Cameron, Charles *Curiosities of Old Edinburgh* (1975) Albyn Press.
Chambers, Robert, *Traditions of Edinburgh* (1847) Edinburgh.
Daily Record 3 July 1970.
Dibdin, Thomas Frognall, *A Bibliographical. Antiquarian and Picturesque Tour in the Counties of England and Scotland* (1838) Vol II.
Country Life 10 December 1954.
Forman, Joan, *Haunted Royal Homes* (1987) Harrap, London.
Evening Dispatch 10 March 1936.
Grant, James, *Cassell's Old and New Edinburgh* (1883) Cassell, Peter Galpin & Co.
Green, Andrew, *Ghosts of Today* (1981) Kaye and Ward.
Holzer, Hans, *Great British Ghost Hunt* (1976) W.H. Allen.
Harries, John, *The Ghost Hunter's Roadbook* (1968) Muller.
Leslie, Shane, *Shane Leslie's Ghost Book* (1955) Hollis & Charter.
Lyal, Adam, *Witchery Tales* (1988) Moubray House Press, Edinburgh.
Magnusson, Magnus, *Scotland: The Story of a Nation* (2001).
Moss, Peter, *Ghosts Over Britain* (1977) Hamish Hamilton.
News Chronicle 2 April 1937.
MacGregor, Alasdair Alpin, *Phantom Footsteps* (1957) Robert Hale.
O'Donnell, Elliot, *Haunted Churches* (1939) Quality Press.
O'Donnell, *Casebook of Ghosts* (1968) Foulsham.
Price, Harry, *Poltergeist Over England* (1945) London.
Proceedings of the Society of Antiquaries of Scotland Vol 12 218; Vol 36 460-3
Robertson, James, *Scottish Ghost Stories* (1996) Warner Books.
Robbins, Rossell Hope, *The Encyclopaedia of Witchcraft and Demonology* (1959) Hamlyn Books.
Scott, Walter, *Letters on Demonology and Witchcraft* (1873) London.
Scottish Daily Mail 25 April 1947.
Shrewsbury, J.F.D, *A History of the Bubonic Plague in the British Isles* (1971) Cambridge University Press.
Sinclair, George, *Satan's Invisible World Discovered* (1808) Edinburgh.
Society for Psychical Research Files; BG14; G477; H160; H192.
Stainton, Moses, *Second Sight: Problems connected with prophetic vision, and records illustrative of the Gift, especially derived from an old work not now available for general use* (1889) London.
Stevens, William Oliver, *Unbidden Guests* (1949) George Allen & Unwin.
Sunday Mail 28 February 1972.
Tales from Scottish Lairds (1981), Jarrolds, Norwich.
Thompson, Francis, *The Supernatural Highlands* (1976) Robert Hale.
Underwood, Peter, *Gazetteer of Scottish and Irish Ghosts* (1974) Souvenir Press.
Wilson, Alan, J, Brogan, Des & McGrail, Frank, *Ghostly Tales and Sinister Stories of Old Edinburgh* (1991).
Wilson, Ian, *Worlds Beyond* (1986).
Weekly Scotsman 9 March 1967.